# HOW TO KEEP YOUR A$$ OUT OF JAIL

KIRBY CLEMENTS JR.

**How to Keep Your A$$ Out of Jail**



This book is for informational purposes only and does not constitute or substitute for obtaining legal advice from a lawyer licensed in your state, as the nuances of the law in your jurisdiction may vary. Anyone reading this book should not rely or act upon the information without seeking professional legal counsel. The reader should consult a lawyer in matters relating to his/her civil or criminal case or concern, particularly with respect to any legal issues that may require immediate consideration or legal attention. No attorney-client relationship is intended or is established by receipt of the information in this book.



Address inquiries to the publisher:
Highest You Publishing
2855 Candler Rd
Suite 10
Decatur, Georgia 30034 USA

Learn more about the author at
www.clementslawgroup.com

ISBN: 978-0-9908257-4-6 (print)
ISBN: 978-0-9908257-0-8 (ebook)

Library of Congress Control Number: 2016917715

Printed in the United States of America

Edited by Annette R. Johnson, Allwrite Communications
Rachel C. Roddy, staff editor

## DEDICATION

To my mom, dad, and wife. My mom and dad paved the way for me. It has been just over a year since we lost my mother, but she instilled a quest for justice in me. My dad is a man of principle. He taught me that you don't have to agree with someone to walk with them. I am where and who I am because of them. Lastly, to my wife, she encouraged me weekly to write a book. She even wrote one to show me how it's done. My parents told me when we were dating that she would always light a fire under me, and they were right. If I did not have her, I'd go get her.

# CONTENTS

# Preface

"The 28-year-old you will hate the 18-year-old you." I have told this to almost all young people who I have counseled when they were getting in trouble. I tell them to think back to when they were a kid and tell me what they wanted to be when they grew up. One client answered me and said that he wanted to be a fire truck when he was a little kid. I asked him if he meant a fireman. His mom said, "No, he wanted to be a fire truck." It turns out that he wore fire truck pajamas, dressed as a fire truck for Halloween, used to run around making fire truck noises all of the time, and pretty much lived as a fire truck.

I asked him, "How would you feel today if your parents had allowed you to make the choice, at 8 years of age, to live as a fire truck, forever? I mean, no matter how old you live to be, you would have to dress as a fire truck, live as a fire truck, make fire truck noises, and do everything that you did at 8 years of age." He looked at me like I was crazy. He agreed with me that in just 10 years, he had changed dramatically and that being a fire truck might keep him from getting girls and make him the butt of many jokes by his friends.

We agreed that in 10 years he had changed dramatically and that it would have been horrible if he had been able to make the permanent decision to live as a fire truck. I went on to say that in 10 more years he was going to be 28. He agreed but wondered where I was going. I finished by telling him that he was making the choice to be known as a criminal. I told him that he would change dramatically in the next 10 years, and that his 28-year-old self would be very angry at the 18-year-old who decided that he would forever be labeled as a criminal. He would have to explain to every employer why he got arrested, and maybe he would be barred from getting certain jobs due to his record. In fact, he was going to continue to have to explain the decisions of an 18-year-old, for the rest of his life.

If you are a young person reading this book, understand that the lessons I am giving you are designed to help you make good decisions. Hopefully, you will understand that there is a very serious legal system that is ready and waiting for people to do something stupid. Don't be that person.

I did NOT write this book to teach anyone how to be a criminal, nor how to be a better criminal nor how to get away with committing crimes. When I give points about individual rights, you must understand that those rights apply to everyone and not just criminals. It just so happens that only people accused of crimes are the ones most likely to be fighting about these rights in court.

Here is some critical news for many people: our criminal justice system really is broken. It is broken in so many ways that I would need a rather lengthy book to explain it. Not everyone who is investigated, arrested, put on trial, convicted or who enters a plea is actually guilty. In fact, there have been high-profile cases where innocent people pled guilty because they were scared of getting longer jail sentences after trial if convicted. They were faced with forced, coerced or false confessions, and flawed police investigations. Add to that a prosecutor who is only focused on winning and who never questioned the police investigation at all. Add to that a judge who would most likely not throw out a confession, and who would, in all likelihood, sentence them to a longer jail term after trial, and these people made the wise choice to plead guilty. Fortunately for some, more evidence emerged that proved their innocence. Even then, they still had to file motions and fight to get their freedom. They needed to understand their rights.

Jail is a place no one wants to go. In fact, I often joke that the word "jail" is Latin for "place that no one wants to go." Not even the people who work there really want to be there. As of 2016, after 26 years of being a lawyer, I have been involved in the criminal process on both sides. I have put people in jail as a prosecutor and fought to keep them out as a defense lawyer. I have taken note of how people end up there. I have noted the mistakes that people made.

I am amazed at how many people facing jail could have avoided the whole process if they had the right information. It is more complex than just telling folks, "Don't break the law." Although American citizens are presumed to know the law, most folks really don't know. This book is going to give you some insight.

This book is designed to give you quick points to avoid breaking the law, as well as provide examples of how the law works. At first, I am going to give you a legal education in just a few short pages. You can skip to ahead if you want to get right to the advice on how to stay out of jail. If you want to understand the basic theory behind the law, then keep reading for a bit. For those of you who want a quick summary of their rights, I do have a quick reference guide. I also give you some examples from real-world cases so that you can see how it all works.

chapter 1

# Mini Law School Education

With the advent of the Internet, information is easily accessible on just about any topic you can imagine. This is especially true in regards to legal and medical issues. Some people who do online research believe they have learned all that they need to know in order to tackle their legal situations. I meet these individuals all the time in my law practice, after they have been arrested or charged with crimes. They call me and declare that their various rights they read about online or saw on a television show were violated. They explain to me how they were representing themselves, but the judge was biased and did not rule for them. I then have to try to undo the damage they've done to their case. Typically, it all falls apart because they had no experience with the actual application of the law. Put rather simply, they messed everything up because they did not know what they were doing. They needed to understand the basics to see how complex the law actually is and why they needed a lawyer all along. After reading this, you will not make that mistake.

## The Constitution and Laws

America is a nation of laws. Our laws start and end with the United States Constitution. It is binding on the federal, state, and local governments. The Constitution has been amended several times and all of those amendments are part of the Constitution. You also have state constitutions and city charters, but the rights guaranteed by them can never be less than what the U.S. Constitution guarantees.

As it relates to any governmental entity in our country, the Constitution is our sword and shield. It allows or forbids governmental action. That governmental action can come in the form of actual laws or the conduct of governmental agents. For the purpose of this book, the agents that we are discussing are law enforcement officers, or the police.

All laws and ordinances passed by legislatures have to comply with the U.S. Constitution. That means that these laws cannot violate the Constitution or our rights under the Constitution. When they are proper, these laws are said to be "constitutional." If they violate it, they are said to be "unconstitutional." The written laws and ordinances are sometimes referred to as "black letter law." That means that they are the actual laws in effect, the actual black letters on the white pages of the law books.

No person can just randomly declare a law unconstitutional or go around conclusively declaring that rights have been violated. A court of law decides whether the Constitution has been violated. Unconstitutional laws cannot be enforced and do not have to be obeyed. To be clear, that is only after a court has declared them unconstitutional and not before.

Actions by governmental agents can also be unconstitutional. You would have to raise the unconstitutionality of their conduct in court as well. That is usually done by way of a lawsuit or by filing a motion. In criminal cases, which are the subject of this book, the challenge to the conduct of law enforcement or to the law is made by filing a motion in the pending case. The court will decide what remedy to apply if the motion is granted.

There are two levels of courts to rule on the constitutionality of government conduct or laws. The first is the **trial court** and the second level is the **appellate court**. Trial courts are where trials take place. The goal is to determine the facts, apply the law, and get a decision or verdict. You usually see trial courts on television with a judge and sometimes a jury. At a trial court, one or both sides are going to call witnesses, present evidence, and make arguments to support or challenge a law or governmental action. The decision of the trial court is called a "ruling" or "judgment." That ruling or judgment can come in the form of an "order" or a "verdict." All that means is that a final decision was made. Trial court rulings only apply to the particular case pending. That means that only the parties in that case have to follow the ruling of the trial court.

A final decision can be appealed, which brings us to the next level: the appellate courts. Those courts do not have juries. They do not have trials. They do not receive new evidence or listen to witnesses. These courts review only the facts that were presented at the trial court level. They review the transcript of the testimony and arguments from the trial court, look at the evidence that was introduced at the trial court, and they may listen to oral arguments by both parties. Oral arguments are like speeches wherein the lawyers get to tell the appellate judges their positions. The appellate judges can ask questions of each side as they consider their decision. Usually more than one appellate judge hears the case. Sometimes it can be as few as three judges or as many as nine, like with the United States Supreme Court. If you think about it, having more judges hear the case makes more sense because their decision has a huge impact. If they decide a law is unconstitutional, then no one has to follow that law, and the Legislature may have to re-write the law. If they reverse a case, it may have to be tried again. Lastly, their decision will also set forth a way of looking at the law that anyone who has a similar issue can use. Their decisions become "case law." Trial courts follow "case law" to help them decide how to apply "black letter law." Thus, these decisions are very significant on many levels and have far-reaching consequences.

In using a sport's analogy, think of it this way. The trial court is where the game is actually played, and a trial judge is the referee. The appellate courts are like the instant replay referees. They look at the film and see what happened and if the rules were applied properly. If they find significant violations, they can order the game to be played again or declare a winner.

There are two main ways that people assert their constitutional rights in court. One way is in the **civil** context, and the other is in the **criminal** context. The goals are different in each. In the former, you want money or an injunction stopping certain behavior. In the latter, you want the case dismissed or evidence suppressed.

In the civil context, a complaining party (the plaintiff) can file a complaint (a lawsuit) against the offending party (the defendant) because of the enforcement of statutes that they believe to be unconstitutional or because of an action by a government agent that violated the Constitution. In this case, the defendant will be the government or its agent. No one goes to jail in the civil context. The relief sought is either money for the constitutional violation or an order banning the unconstitutional activity.

In criminal cases, constitutional issues are not stated as lawsuits. They are spelled out in a motion. In these situations, the claim is that police conduct violated the Constitution and that the evidence seized should be excluded. The defendant may also claim that their punishment is "cruel and unusual" in violation of the Constitution. They might also claim that the law that they are accused of violating is unconstitutional or being applied against them in an unconstitutional manner. Lastly, they might allege that their statutory rights were violated during the trial in some manner.

In addition to raising constitutional violations, a person can file an appeal with an appellate court claiming that the trial court got it wrong or that some error took place that should result in a reversal. If you have watched television trials, you often see one lawyer say the word, "Objection." When an objection is made, the lawyer is saying, "Hey, this is wrong." The judge can either say "sustained" or "overruled." If the judge sustains the objection, it means that he or she agrees that a mistake happened, and it should stop. If the judge overrules the objection, he or she is saying that there is nothing wrong with what is happening. On appeal, the losing lawyer can argue that the judge made a mistake ruling against him or her on the objection.

An appellate court can issue a number of different types of rulings. Sometimes the appellate court can issue a ruling that settles the matter. In effect, they just correct the trial court. For example, if the defendant claims that the evidence was insufficient to convict him, the appellate court could agree. In that case, they would reverse the conviction, and that would end the matter. The defendant could not be tried again because the Double Jeopardy clause of the Constitution does not allow anyone to be tried twice if the evidence was insufficient to convict him or her the first time. Other times, they reverse the trial court and send the case back for the trial judge to fix. Thus, if a judge imposes a cruel and unusual punishment, the Eighth Amendment is violated, the sentence is reversed, and a new one has to be imposed. If the trial court allows evidence into the case that should have been excluded, the appeals court will reverse that case, and the trial will have to start all over again.

So there you have the court process. You start with the trial court and fight about what the facts are, what facts are admissible into evidence, which witness is to be believed, and what laws apply. After that, you can appeal to decide if those facts supported the judgment, if the facts should have been admitted, and if the law was applied correctly. Notice that on appeal, the issue is never going to be whether the witnesses should have been believed.

One last thing, and it is a huge thing. When the appellate court looks at a case, it is looking to support or affirm a judgment. The law does not like endless litigation, and it does not like re-litigation. The law favors finality of judgments. As a result, the party filing the appeal has an uphill battle to win. You are not guaranteed a trial free from error; you are guaranteed a trial free from the kind of errors that call into question the validity of the judgment. If the law was misapplied, then the judgment is questionable and should be reversed. If evidence was admitted that should not have been admitted, then that probably affected the jury verdict and a new trial is ordered. It is very complicated, which is why it is better to have a lawyer at the trial stage. It's even better to never have to be in court in the first place. It is really important to not help the state in prosecuting the case by giving them evidence to use against you at the investigative stage.

## Evidence in Its Many Forms

Evidence comes in two basic categories: **direct** and **circumstantial** (indirect). Direct evidence clearly *proves* its point. This is eyewitness testimony or video that expressly declares who or what was involved. Circumstantial evidence suggests or infers its point. It is more like a clue and includes all forms of evidence except direct eyewitness testimony. For example, if you see it is actually raining, that would be direct evidence of rain. On the other hand, if you woke up and saw that everything outside was wet, that would be circumstantial evidence. In my example, while the wet ground is circumstantial evidence that it rained, the truth might be that someone turned on the sprinklers. People tend to put more faith in direct evidence because there is less room for other explanations.

In addition, to those two basic kinds, evidence can also come in two basic forms: **tangible** and **intangible** evidence. **Tangible evidence** is something you can touch. You could call it actual "things" or "stuff," but the fancy word is "tangible." This book is tangible. A pen is tangible. Drugs are tangible. A murder weapon is tangible. There is also **intangible evidence**. This can be statements, confessions, opinions, observations, identifications, or anything where there is not an actual thing. An example of this can be someone saying they smelled burning marijuana. At present, no one can box up that smell and bring it to court months later. Instead, they can say, "I smelled burning marijuana." So, it would be the intangible evidence of the smell and the person's opinion that it was marijuana. I like to say that you can't touch intangible evidence, but you can talk about it.

Evidence also includes documents and photographs. They are tangible pieces of evidence because you can touch them, but they reveal things that you talk about. Thus, they have an intangible nature. A picture shows you how something looks, and a document shows you what someone said. Think of it like this: they could take a photo of the scene to show you how dark it was and how messy it was, but you can't touch dark or messy. You can touch the photo and talk about what it shows.

Now, circumstantial and direct evidence can be described as either tangible or intangible. For example, in a DUI case, a police officer might testify, "I smelled the odor of an alcoholic drink coming from the defendant, and he could not stand up straight." The **intangible evidence** was that he smelled an alcoholic beverage. This was **circumstantial** because he was of the *opinion* that it was an alcoholic beverage based on the odor and how the defendant was acting, despite never having seen the defendant take a drink. The **direct evidence** was that he *saw* that the defendant could not stand up straight. It gets pretty complicated. In the end, whether it is circumstantial or direct evidence, tangible or intangible, it will all be used to convict the man of drunk driving. All types of evidence gets considered.

You can be convicted based only on circumstantial evidence. You can be convicted based only on direct evidence. You can be convicted based on a combination of direct and circumstantial evidence. How strong the case is may vary, but in the end, any combination is enough to convict someone. People have been convicted of murder where no body was ever found. They have been convicted of aggravated assault where there was no weapon found. It is all about how a jury or judge views the evidence and which witness they believe.

The goal of the government is to get as much evidence before the court as possible that supports their claim that a defendant is guilty. The accused, on the other hand, is hoping to keep as much of that evidence out as possible. The only way for the accused to do that is to claim that there was a violation of the law or Constitution.

## Understanding Your Basic Rights

If evidence is seized in violation of your constitutional rights, that evidence should be excluded from the case. Thus, your basic rights are as follows:

1. You have the right to be free from an *unreasonable* search and seizure. That comes from the Fourth Amendment to the Constitution. In this regard, the law recognizes three levels of police-citizen encounters. At each level of encounter, the scope of what is reasonable changes. As we move up to higher levels, the more authority the police have. One can go up the levels or down the levels. You can start at level one and quickly go up to level three. You can start on level two and go down to level one. As facts develop, levels can change. The simple way to think about it is as follows: what is reasonable for police to do at a higher level is probably unreasonable at a lower level, but what is reasonable for police to do at a lower level will always be reasonable at a higher level.

a. Level one — This is the *casual encounter.* You are free to terminate the encounter at will. If the police ask you to "come here" and are just asking questions, you can end the encounter. They can come to your front door, knock and ask to talk to you. You can refuse, however. They can wave you over to them to ask you questions. You don't have to like it, but they can ask. They can ask if you committed any crimes. The point is that they cannot be coercive or compel you to continue with this encounter. They cannot require that you submit to a search or a pat down or compel you to answer questions. They can ask you to consent to those things, but you can refuse. The police do not have to tell you that you have the right to remain silent or the right to have an attorney present during any questioning.

b. Level two — This is the brief *investigatory detention.* You are not under arrest, but you are not free to leave. (We will talk about your rights during any police encounter later on.) At this level encounter, the police have an articulable suspicion of something being amiss. There does not have to be an actual crime, just a reasonable suspicion that something is wrong. For example, if you came home and three strangers came from around the back of your house, you would want the police to stop them and hold them there until they make sure that there were no signs of forced entry into your house. While the police were detaining the strangers and doing a quick check to make sure that no windows were broken, the people would not be free to leave, but they would also not be under arrest. They would be held in a brief investigatory detention. Maybe they were just cutting through yards or looking for a lost dog. On the other hand, they could have been looking in your window to see what they could steal. In either event, the police could detain them to figure out what was going on with them. They still can't search you, but they may be able to pat you down (outer garments) for weapons for their own safety. They can ask you questions about crimes they suspect you to have committed or ask you to do sobriety tests, but they don't have to tell you that you have the right to remain silent or that you have the right to have an attorney during any questioning. You can't end this encounter. You cannot walk away. As you read my rules, you will understand what to do during these encounters.

c. Level three — This is an arrest. Either the words, "you're under arrest" or the actions by the officers make it clear to a reasonable person that this detention is not temporary. Let's consider the earlier example of the police stopping the people who came from behind your house. During the investigatory detention, the police start asking them questions, and each one gives a different story. One guy says that they were taking a short cut through your yard. The other guy says that they were looking for a lost dog. The third guy does not say anything. As the police investigate, they find footprints in your grass near your back door and footprints near your rear windows. At this point, the officer has probable cause to believe a crime was committed. He tells the strangers that he is arresting them for trespassing. At that point, they are under arrest. Maybe the officer tells the third guy that his friends are telling different stories, and the third guy takes off running. The police handcuff the other two and put them in the back of their cars. When the police catch the third guy, it will be clear that he is under arrest, even if they don't say the words. There are hosts of ways that an encounter can become a level three. It depends on the circumstances, but the key point is that if it is clear that you are not free to leave and that this is not a temporary detention, then it is an arrest. You cannot walk away from a level three encounter. They can search you at level three. They can search your things as well. If they question you about the crime, they must inform you that you have the right to remain silent and you have the right to have a lawyer present for any questioning.

2. You have the right to remain silent and not make any statements to the police. That comes from the Fifth Amendment. Most everybody knows this, but for some reason, so many people do not know how to shut up. We will talk about this later.
3. You have the right to have a lawyer present during police questioning. That also comes from the Fifth Amendment.
4. You have the right to have a lawyer assist you in defense to a prosecution. That comes from the Sixth Amendment.

Here is the problem for the average person: knowing when to exercise those rights and knowing when those rights apply. The rights that I listed are the rights that most often are litigated in a criminal case. Evidence can be excluded if the police violate these rights. Understanding the rules and exceptions to those rules takes years of experience and still depends on what facts come out in court. In a few sentences, let me show you how complex this can get.

You don't have the right to be free from search and seizure, only unreasonable search and seizure. A pat down or frisk for weapons is not a search. Maybe the police were doing a pat down for weapons when they found something on you that resembled a weapon. Worse for you, when they patted you down, they could tell from the feel of an object, that it was contraband, and now they can seize it and arrest you. Well, more rules apply and more questions have to be asked to see if the pat down or frisk was justifiable. We have to ask (1) why they stopped you; (2) what level encounter was this; (3) why they felt the need to pat you down; (4) was this a pat down or was it really a search; (5) if it was a pat down, did it go too far; (6) if it was search, was it unreasonable? There are so many questions to be asked, and your freedom depends upon the answers.

Once you are in custody and the police are interrogating you, they have to tell you of your right to remain silent and to have a lawyer. The question is when are you legally in custody? A brief detention is not custody. If you are not in custody, then they don't have to tell you that you have the right to remain silent even though you still have the right to remain silent. If you are not in custody, they don't have to tell you that you have the right to a lawyer even though you still have the right to have a lawyer prior to answering any police interrogation.

Even if you are in custody, they don't have to tell you any rights if they don't plan on interrogating you. If they ask you a question and you start making incriminating statements, attorneys have to see if their questions constituted interrogation? Interrogation is defined as questioning that is likely to lead to an incriminating response. Of course, for example, they may not know that the question "where are you coming from" might result in you telling them that you just left a crime scene. On the other hand, if they are stopping you because they think that you are coming from the crime scene, then that question would be considered interrogation unless it was during a brief investigatory detention to see if you are the person they suspect of leaving the crime scene. Maybe you are in custody on one thing and they are asking you about something else. Well, you are not in custody on the new investigation, so should they tell you of your right to remain silent? As you can see, it really gets very complex.

I can tell you without hesitation that no officer is going to come into court and testify that he violated your right to be free from an unreasonable search and seizure. No officer is going to say that he deprived you of your right to a lawyer. The judge is going to listen to the evidence related to any motion that you file and then decide if they think that your rights were violated. If you lose, you can file an appeal, but as I said earlier, it is an uphill battle to win on appeal.

These rules are designed to keep you from giving the powerful government any more help to target you for criminal prosecution. In short, I am not going to teach you how to commit a crime. I am not going to teach you how to conceal criminal activity. I am going to give you universal points that explain your rights and also criminal law and rules. These rules vary a bit from state to state, but the principle remains fairly constant.

Before we begin with my rules, I want to take some time to talk about the justice system. I often tell people that getting caught up in the criminal process is like falling into a muddy hole. No one gets out clean. Think about that!

chapter 2

# The Justice System

I was on trial with a young attorney who made a very profound statement about our American justice system in his closing argument to the jury. He said, "The American justice system is terrible. It is full of flaws. It allows for bias to prevail. It wrongfully convicts people. Money can have an undue influence. The poor don't get as much justice as the rich. It is really a terrible system. It is also *the best* system that the world has ever known. There is none better."

Our system has its flaws. The issue is how people can best position themselves to withstand the rigors, flaws and disadvantages in our system.

## Harsh Realities about Our Justice System

While our justice system has many good, honest people working in it who do difficult jobs, the system also has long-standing problems. I am going to point out its flaws, but don't take that to mean that the system is all bad. Good or bad, you don't want to get caught up in the justice system.

1. **It is not fair.** I don't care what anyone tells you, it is not fair. You are at a financial disadvantage. You do not have as much money as the government when it comes to a criminal case. They will outspend you every single time. Being a defendant means that no one really cares about you and thinks that you get what you deserve. No one gets mad at a judge who favors the prosecutor, but they always trash judges who do anything that seems as if they are soft or fair to the accused. They make you post bond to get out of jail to fight your charges, and there goes the money that you could use for your defense. The grand jury process, whereby you are formally charged with a crime in a document called an "indictment," happens in secret, is run by the prosecutor, and has very few rules governing it. It has been said that "the prosecution could indict a ham sandwich," and that is pretty much true. The grand jury is virtually a rubber stamp for the prosecutor. If they want to charge you, they can, for the most part.
2. **They try to break you mentally.** Prosecutors try to keep you in jail even if they know that they are going to offer you probation. Seriously, it makes no sense to argue for a person to spend money on bail on a case that is really a probation case or a minimal amount of jail time. They understand that if you have been sitting in jail for three months and the offer is probation, you will probably take it even if you are innocent. The jail conditions under which pre-trial detainees are held are terrible. It is like prison before prison. They have to eat jail food, which is mysterious at times. They only eat when they get fed, and that can be as little as twice a day. Ask folks who have been held at the local jail how they like the mystery meat sandwiches. Eating poorly prepared, barely nutritious meals will break your spirit. Furthermore, prisoners

are shuttled about and treated like the worst people in society, and they have just been accused of a crime, not convicted. If you are out on bond, they will make you have to come to court over and over again for calendar calls, even when they know that nothing is going to happen on your case. Try having to explain to your boss why you needed so much time off. Some people actually lose their job, and that begins an entire financial avalanche for them.

3. **Judges have biases.** Judges are just people. When I was a prosecutor, we used to know which judges were "good judges for us." When the defense used to file a motion, I would not argue the law, I'd say, "My judge is not going to grant that motion." I've even had prosecutors say it to me now that I am a defense lawyer. Plea negotiations sometime hinge on who the judge happens to be. When the lawyers know that the judge is harsh when it comes to sentencing, the best thing the defense might have to do is take a negotiated plea that is still harsher than they feel the case deserves. This means the prosecutor has a lot of power. I've only seen a few that are so-called "defense judges." When I say a few, I mean perhaps five in 26 years!
4. **Pressure is used that discourages trials.** You are not supposed to be punished for going to trial, but case law says that if you go to trial and are convicted, you can be sentenced harsher than the last plea offer. That really discourages people from going to trial. Maybe you agree that you did one crime but not another. If the prosecution will not dismiss the charge that you dispute and you go to trial and win on that charge but still lose on the ones you agreed that you violated, you can get more jail time than was offered before trial. That pressure makes trial a huge risk.

5. **Police who lie are rarely exposed.** When you find out a police officer has a disciplinary history a mile long or it is common knowledge amongst defense lawyers that a particular cop stretches the truth, nothing happens to the cop. They will keep on using him or her. I've only known of one prosecutor who has worked to get those cops fired and worked to keep them out of law enforcement. That particular prosecutor is a tough, hard-nosed guy, and he takes the rules seriously. You would think that knowing there are "problem" officers out there, which could lead to miscarriages of justice, would motivate prosecutors to try to get rid of them. I've not seen it happen except in the most egregious of cases. A lazy cop can be trained; a lying cop can ruin someone's life. There is a big difference.
6. **Money, social status, and race matter.** People at the top of the socio-economic ladder who commit crimes, unless it is newsworthy, are more apt to get better treatment. If you are poor, lower class, don't look a certain way, well, too bad for you. The poor, minorities, and poor minorities are treated like they are criminals. Those who look less "criminal" get treated like they made a "mistake." It is not a guarantee, but it is an advantage.

   I had a case where my client looked a bit "rough" and had recently purchased a car from a mechanic. It turned out that the mechanic actually owned a "chop shop" where he disassembled stolen cars and sold the parts or built a new car. He had duped my client, who had cooperated with the police, but they still arrested him. He showed them all of the documentation that he had been given and then went to the local police department near the shady mechanic to report that he had been scammed. When I spoke to the prosecutor, I offered to give her all of the documentation and asked her to contact the other police department. Without seeing a thing, she said to me, "I don't believe your client." I asked how could she say that without even seeing the evidence or speaking to the police officer. She replied, "I just don't believe your client." I pointed out that all she had was a police report and my client's booking photo. She said, "It does not matter. I just don't believe him." To make a long story short, she ended up having to dismiss the case. Amazingly, she was unhappy, as she conceded that the evidence could not support a conviction.

7. **Selective law enforcement happens.** Everyone knows it, and it is allowed. That's right. Police will target certain racial groups for enforcement, meaning more traffic stops, more searches, more frisks, more interrogations, etc. It is allowed because as long as they can say that you committed a crime, nothing else really matters. Let that sink in for a moment. They can and do target certain groups of people and ignore others committing the same or similar crimes. It's legal. It is not a defense that they only stopped you because you were a minority, if you were breaking the law. They stopped you because you were a minority breaking the law. The "breaking the law" part is all that matters.
8. **They will do what it takes to win.** The law does not guarantee you an error-free trial, just a "fair" one. This means that prosecutors can intentionally violate certain rules. The issue will be if it was a "harmless error." Many things are considered to be "harmless" errors, and prosecutors know this. The motto I learned as a prosecutor was this: "There can be no appeal without a conviction." This means to win first, and then worry about the appeal. The appellate court may even condemn the prosecutor's activity, but they may not reverse the conviction.

With that last point, I want you to understand that getting caught up in an investigation can be relatively easy. Now that you understand how the criminal process works between trial and appeal, you know what you are facing when you get to court. The only thing that you can control is what evidence they get from you. Don't help them make a case against you.

## Police Tricks that Work All the Time

Police officers are supposed to act on information. The information can come from you, someone else, their own observations, or any combination of all of that. Once they get enough information, they can arrest you. Here are some tricks they use:

1. They ask you, "Do you know why I'm here?" or "Do you know why I stopped you?" If you say "yes," well you just confirmed their information that you did something wrong. That will be used against you. When confronted by this, you can say, "I'd rather you tell me." Never admit anything. You don't know why they are there. You are not a mind reader. If you do know why they are there, well, you probably should shut up anyway.
2. They tell you that someone said that you did something and then ask you about it. You don't have to answer. It does not have to be true. It usually goes something like this: "X told me that you hit him. What's going on?" If you really were the victim, maybe telling your story makes sense. On the other hand, if there is a question as to whether you or X is the victim, you might want to not answer any questions.
3. They ask, "Where are the drugs?" or "Where is the stuff?" Shut up. Of course, you should not have any drugs in

the first place. Seriously, if you have drugs, you probably should go to jail or rehab. Saying "I only have a little bit of weed" is not going to keep you from going to jail. It will get you on the express bus to the local jail.

## Acceptable Police Tactics

1. **You fit the description.** The police can and should stop you to investigate you if you fit the description. Descriptions are sometimes pretty general, and criminals fleeing the scene can move quickly. Thus, police can stop anyone that fits the general description if they have "reasonable suspicion." It could be just race, approximate age, sex, and direction of travel. If that is all they have, they can't make up more. If you fit the description, they can conduct a brief investigative stop.
2. **Police deception is fine.** The police can lie, mislead, create false impressions, be confusing, and all of that. Let's be serious, how many crimes do you think they would solve if they told the truth on everything. They would only catch the dumbest criminals out there.
3. **Psychological tactics are fine.** Playing "good cop, bad cop" is fine. Invading your personal space to make you feel uncomfortable is fine. Pressing your buttons is fine. Not treating you with the level of respect that you think that you are due is perfectly acceptable. Look, police officers are not out there to make friends. They are out there to solve crimes and catch criminals. It is a tough job done by brave people.
4. **They don't have to go above and beyond.** Case law dictates when an officer has to tell you your rights. Until that point, they don't have to tell you. They don't have

to make sure that you understand the scope of your rights. In other words, they don't they have to explain your rights; they just have to alert you to them. They are investigating you; they are not your lawyers.

Below is a basic chart that summarizes the constitutional rights involved throughout the legal process. Despite the size of the chart, there is actually a huge amount of case law involved to explain the nuances of each situation.

| PHASE | WHAT THEY NEED | CONSTITUTIONAL RIGHTS |
|---|---|---|
| **Casual Encounter** | No reason needed<br>Encounter can't be coercive | 4th Amendment:<br>You can end the encounter |
| **Brief Investigatory Detention** | Reasonable articulable suspicion:<br>Be able to say what was suspicious even if not a crime | 4th Amendment<br>They should only investigate whatever caused them to detain you. |
| **Arrest** | Probable Cause:<br>Reasonably believed that a crime was committed and you were involved | 4th and 5th Amendment<br>You have right to remain silent |
| **Pre-Trial** | State bears burden of proof | 4th, 5th, 6th Amendment<br>Right to a lawyer (get one) |
| **Trial** | Proof beyond a reasonable doubt | 5th, 6th, and 14th Amendment |

Remember, you always have the right to remain silent. You NEVER have to answer police questions, especially because what you say can be used against you. Well, giving your name and address is a good idea. No need to argue about why they are asking your name unless you just want to.

chapter 3

# Keeping Your A$$ Out Of Jail

## QUICK REFERENCE GUIDE

1. **You never have to answer questions by the police.** You do have to produce identification if you are driving. See your state's "black letter law" as to identification rules in general.
    a. You don't have to say where you are coming from.
    b. You don't have to say how you know the people with you.
    c. You don't have to say where you are going.
    d. You don't have to say if you've been drinking, even if you smell like you took a bath in liquor.
    e. You don't have to admit to smoking or having marijuana, even if the smell is strong and you have some.
    f. You don't have to explain why you don't want to answer questions.
    g. You don't have to explain anything.

h. You don't have to do sobriety tests.
i. You can refuse to take breath tests.

2. **You don't have to agree to be searched if you are NOT under arrest or they don't have a search warrant.** You can refuse. If they go ahead, just make sure that you say out loud that you are refusing.
   a. You don't have to agree to let them look in your stuff, so that you can leave. They can't condition you leaving on your being searched.
   b. You don't have to agree that they can frisk you.
   c. You don't have to open the trunk.
   d. You don't have to let them in your house without a warrant.
   e. You don't have to let them know that something belongs to you.
   f. You don't have to sign any consent to search.

3. **Don't be rude. Just be clear. Here are things that you can say.**
   a. I don't want you to search me. I'm not resisting, but I don't consent.
   b. I don't want you to frisk me. I'm not resisting, but I don't consent.
   c. I don't want you searching anything. I'm not resisting but I don't consent.
   d. I don't want to answer any questions, thank you.
      i. I don't want to answer any questions without a lawyer.
      ii. I'll call a lawyer and let them speak for me.
      iii. I will give you my identification.
   e. I don't want to remain here, can I leave. I want to leave right now.

4. **Don't be intimidated. If they are going to arrest you, focus on defense.**
    a. If they say they are going to arrest you if you don't answer the question, and the question seeks more than your name and address, don't give in to the pressure. Tell them you want a lawyer and invoke your Fifth Amendment right to "remain silent."
    b. If they say that they are going to arrest you if you don't perform the sobriety tests, don't give in to the pressure. You can never pass the tests. They are just gathering evidence to use against you.
    c. If they say that they are going to arrest you if you don't let them search you or your things, don't give in to the pressure. Just tell them, like I wrote above, that you don't' consent, want to leave, and will not physically resist. Your lawyer can move to suppress the evidence later.
    d. If they say that they are going to arrest you if you don't shut up, tell them that you will shut up, but that you are not consenting to being there and want to leave right away.

5. **Don't be stupid with the police.**
    a. If they tell you to move back, do it and don't get close.
    b. If they tell you to be quiet, do it. Arguing never helps.
    c. If they tell you go away, do it. Your whole goal is to leave on your own and with your freedom. If anyone with you is not following the rules, then too bad for him or her. You can only save yourself.
    d. Don't break the law. It really is just that simple. It is hard to understand how anyone could actually not get this. Keep your hands to yourself, leave peo-

ple's stuff alone, don't act a fool, and stay away from drugs and weapons.

e. If you don't like being told what to do and think that no one can tell you what to do, you are just plain wrong. They will get as many police as needed to arrest you. The jail will hold you. The judge will tell you where you will spend the next few years of your life. The prison correctional officers will tell you when and where to eat, sleep, bathe, use the bathroom, wake up, and go home. Control yourself or someone else will.

6. **Get a lawyer.**

   a. If you are thinking about talking to the police about a crime you are possibly involved in, get a lawyer.
   b. If you have a case coming up in court, get a lawyer.
   c. If you have been to court and have another date coming up get a lawyer.
   d. If you are thinking about taking a plea on a case, get a lawyer.
   e. If you don't like the lawyer you have, don't trust him, don't think he knows what he is doing, then get another lawyer first.

# THE EASY RULES

# Don't break the law!

It seems pretty simple, but so many people do it. You can't hit people, take their stuff, use drugs, drive recklessly, violate people's rights, or lie in certain situations. As I learned in grade school, "keep your hands to yourself, leave their stuff alone, and tell the truth." If you can't do this, jail is in your future. Most people learned this rule in the first grade. If you missed that day, here is your reminder.

2

# Don't break the law with other people

If for some reason you just cannot follow rule number one, then don't break the law with other people. One of you is the crazy fool who will end up hurting some innocent person and making it worse for everyone. A group of criminals is just a bunch of concentrated fools. If something is about to go down, just walk away. Your friends may end up changing their minds and not doing the crime. If you all go ahead and do it, then one of you is going to be the snitch. Let me tell you a secret; every defense attorney tells his client that if he snitches, he can get the client a better a deal. The smart client takes the deal.

# Don't use a weapon

If you are dedicated to committing a crime, at least make this one good decision. Here is a fact: if you hurt someone, they will look for you longer and harder than if you didn't. If you kill someone, they will never stop looking for you. There is no statute of limitations on murder. Crime happens and that is sad. Violent crime is just ridiculous. If you, your friend, or the guy you just met is armed with a weapon, nothing but bad things are going to happen. Don't do it. If someone takes a gun to a fight, it is likely going to get used. Don't take one with you so you can avoid the temptation. A weapon, for those who are just hell-bent on committing a crime, is anything that can be used to hurt someone. Ask yourself this question now, before you ask it for the next 30 years in your jail cell, "Is this worth life in prison?" I'm hoping you responded, "No." If you did not, then I am surprised that you are reading this book.

# Breaking rules 1, 2, or 3 pretty much mean that you are headed for jail

Honestly, I don't know why you would want to break those rules, but some folks just have that inner criminal waiting to get out. Hopefully, that is not you.

# Destroying evidence or concealing it is a crime

If you are trying to hide evidence from the police, or you try to destroy evidence, then you are going to jail. Maybe they can't prove that you did the crime they were investigating, but they can prove that you destroyed evidence. If you try to swallow the weed, that is tampering. If you toss it out the window, that is tampering. Tampering is also circumstantial evidence that you were committing whatever crime they were investigating. By the way, if the cop sees you trying to eat the drugs, it is reasonable for him to grab you by the throat and force you to spit it out. That's right; they can choke it right out of you. As a side note, what goes in will come out. If you actually swallow it, they can wait for it to come out. They have special toilets and everything.

# Running or hiding is evidence of guilt

Guilty people run and don't want to get caught. If a jury hears that you were running or hiding, they will think that you did it because you are guilty. In a tier one casual contact with police you can end the encounter at will, running away is fine. Of course, if you run they are going to chase you. Its habit. As the song from "The Wiz" says, "ease on down the road." On the other hand, if the police are investigating you for suspicious activity or have arrested you, you can't run away. The easiest way to decide if you can leave is to ask. Just ask if you are free to leave and state that you want to leave and do not want to continue the encounter. Of course, if they stopped you with the blue lights on, you are not free to leave. If they chased you down, you are not free to leave. If you are in handcuffs, you are not free to leave. If you are the passenger in a car that has been stopped, let them know that you don't want to stay and ask if you are free to leave. The bottom line, if it does not look like you have done anything wrong or you have been ruled out as a suspect, ask to leave. Walk away.

## PERSONAL OBSERVATIONS

So many of these first six rules should go without saying, but after 26 years of practicing law, it needs to be said. Don't do it; don't do it with people; and don't do it with a weapon. If you did it, destroying evidence or running is just like screaming out, "I'm guilty." There is no right way to do the wrong thing. There is no best way to break the law. Still, you might find yourself on the wrong end of an investigation or prosecution. If that happens, well, hopefully you will have followed the next rules that I give you. They will help keep your butt out of jail.

# TALKING (AKA RUNNING YOUR MOUTH)

# You have the right to remain silent

Use it. Shut up. Name, date of birth, and address, that's it. After that, you are just asking for trouble. Seriously, what could you possibly have to say that will help you? YOU DO NOT HAVE TO ANSWER QUESTIONS DURING ANY POLICE QUESTIONING. Remember, when we spoke about the three tiers of police encounters — tier one, two or three? Well, no matter what tier you are in, you have the constitutional right to "remain silent." USE IT. Let me tell you a secret. When I was a prosecutor, I did not care what a suspect said. If they confessed or made admissions, then that was great! It was an easy conviction. If they lied, then they were locked in that lie and could not change. If they tried to change stories, I'd just ask the jury not to believe them at all. Were they lying when they first spoke or were they lying at trial? Either way, they were lying. The point is shut up. Invoke your Fifth

Amendment and shut up. If you did something wrong, shut up. If they think you did something wrong, shut up. Name, address, driver's license, and then shut up. Notice how I keep saying to "shut up"? Of course, if you were not involved in anything, deny any wrongdoing, and then shut up.

# 8

# Don't try to be smart

You can talk yourself into an arrest. I know, I know, you think that you are so smart. You just can't resist trying to lie your way out of the situation or smart talk the officer. You have mastered the art of talking smart to your parents. You are the class clown when it comes to mouthing off to teachers. Well, mom, dad, and the principal can't put you in jail. The police can. Keep talking and they will. Maybe you want to be cute and witty. You don't know if what you are saying is confirming parts of their case. You may be smart mouthing yourself right into prison. Also, they will use your smart mouth answers against you in court. Therefore, shut up. I hope that you are noticing a theme here. Invoke your constitutional right to a lawyer and to remain silent, and then be silent.

# Loud mouths get special attention

Keep your attitude to yourself. Maybe you are mad because the officer is getting under your skin. So what?! They are trained to do that. They get under your skin, insult you in sneaky ways, or disrespect you. If you lose your cool, you may then lose your freedom. Shut up. This is actually one of the oldest tricks that some cops use. They invade your personal space, tell you to shut up, mock you, and ask questions that are phrased in a way that twists what you said. Maybe you are offended because you feel that you have been stopped because of your race or because you fit the description. If you get mad and do something stupid or say something stupid, they win. It is a trick and a trap. Don't fall for it. Shut up and keep your cool. If you get the urge to curse out the cop, then you must also have the urge to go to jail. Most places make it a crime to use "fighting words." Those are words that are designed to incite people to violence. If you call the cop a son of a b****, those words are fighting words, and you are getting arrested and searched. If you are not sure what you can't say, let's just say if it involves name-calling, threats, promises, or insults, then simply shut up. If your friend is mouthing off, tell your friend to "shut up."

10

# Tell it to your lawyer

If you have a guilty conscience and want to confess, then confess to your lawyer. If you want to confess to the police, do it with your lawyer present. An attorney can make sure that your words are put in the proper context. Otherwise, shut up. If you are under arrest, you need a lawyer. If you are the target of an investigation, you need a lawyer. The police will tell you that you can tell your side of the story. Tell them that you are getting a lawyer and then shut up. The police will tell you all the evidence that they have and ask what you have to say. You will respond that you want to talk to a lawyer first. The police will promise you that they are just trying to clear some things up. Well, if those things involve you and a crime, then you need a lawyer. Here is a little nugget for you: there is rarely ever any reason that a lawyer would let his client confess to a crime. I don't care if you feel bad. Get help with your feelings in counseling. If you want to confess, wait until after your lawyer tells you what the consequences are.

# 11

# Never admit to anything

That means shut up. Admissions are kind of like confessions, but different. A confession says, "I did it." An admission says, "I was there when it happened" or "I am connected to it." An admission plus other evidence equals jail. This is why having a lawyer is so important. Maybe you want to admit to being with someone *before* the crime happened, but the police take it to mean that you were with them when the crime happened. Having a lawyer present could have prevented that mix up. Trust me, the police are not going to help you clear it up. They need to close their case. You usually won't know when you are making admissions because you don't know what the police know. By admitting to being with a certain person, for example, you may have admitted to being with the main criminal. Imagine if your friends just robbed a store and then pick you up. Later, the police stop you all and ask you what you did earlier. For some reason, you just can't keep your mouth shut or ask for a lawyer, so you start talking. You say, "I was with my friends." Well, there you go... to jail. Your friends were involved in a robbery earlier, and you just admitted to being with them. You protest, saying, "Oh, no, officer, you misunderstood me. I was with them after they did whatever you say they did."

"Me too," says each of the other people. Yeah, who would have thought that criminals would lie to save themselves? Just ask for a lawyer and shut up.

# No, you will not just come down to the station

Sometimes a detective will call you and as you to come down to talk. Maybe they need to clear things up or hear your side of the story. Do not ever agree to go down to the precinct to "clear things up" or "tell your side of the story." If they want you to come down, you have problems. You are NOT going to talk yourself out of getting arrested. If they want to talk to you, it is because they are investigating you and are going to arrest you whether you talk or not. Get a lawyer to intervene. There may be reasons to talk, but until you have a lawyer to discuss everything with you, there is no reason that you should talk. Better safe than sorry. Of course, if you had absolutely nothing to do with anything, you may want to tell your story. You know what you did or did not do.

# 13

# "But they might arrest me if I don't talk."

Sometimes the police will tell you that if you don't come in and talk to them, they are just going to get a warrant. Well, here is a newsflash. They were going to get one anyway. In fact, they might already have one. Seriously, do not fall for this threat. I had an officer tell me that if my client did not talk, he was going to arrest her. Well, she did not talk. When she turned herself in, I looked at the date on the arrest warrant. They had gotten the warrant before they had asked her to speak. They had lied to us. Yes, the police can lie to you.

# Here are some tricky questions that they ask:

a. They will ask, "Is there anything I should know about?" If you say, "Yes," you have admitted that you know about and are possibly involved in whatever crime they are investigating. You should say, "I choose to remain silent, and I am not answering any questions like that."
b. After you refuse to answer a question, they say, "So, you are telling me you have something to hide?" You respond, "No, I am invoking my constitutional right to remain silent."
c. They may try the guilt trip: "If you have not done anything wrong, then you have nothing to fear." Then you reply, "I am exercising my constitutional right to remain silent."
d. They may ask you, "Do you know why I am here?" There is no right way to answer that question. If you say "yes," you admit that you were involved in the wrongdoing, assuming someone called them on you. If you say "no," they will

say that you were trying to lie. The best answer I have heard is to say, "I'd rather you tell me why you are here."

e. They may tell you that if you tell them who else was involved, then you can go home. That is a lie. Not true. False. They just figured you committed the crime with other people. You need a lawyer.

15

# When in doubt, always invoke your Fifth Amendment right to remain silent and consult an attorney

This is a nice fancy way of saying shut up. That is a theme here.

# SPECIAL CASES

## Loud Mouth's Get Special Attention

Jerry was driving his new car with his friend Dan. Jerry was busy changing the radio and did not notice that he was weaving down the roadway. He also did not notice Officer Phillips had pulled up behind him. After watching him weave a few times, Officer Phillips pulled the car over, as he wanted to investigate why Jerry was weaving.

Jerry explained to the officer that he was changing the radio and was not aware that he had crossed the center line. The officer told him that he had not crossed the line, but he had been weaving inside of his lane. Officer Phillips said that he needed to confirm that Jerry's license and insurance were in order. Dan, who had been drinking, decided that he did not believe the officer's reasons for stopping them. Dan started getting loud with the officer. Jerry kept telling Dan to "chill," but Dan had been reading online about police stops. Dan felt that this was improper, and he was going to make the officer regret pulling them over. He began to insult the officer and was getting more hostile by the moment.

Officer Phillips called for backup and several officers arrived. By this point, Dan began to call the officers names, insulted their mothers and generally went off on them calling them "pigs" and "idiots." What Dan did not know was that his loud behavior and insults were against the local disorderly conduct ordinance.

Once he was taken out of the car, they smelled the alcohol on his breath and asked him if he had been drinking, to which he said, "Yes." Dan, who was 20 years old at the time, was arrested for disorderly conduct and underage possession of alcohol. When they searched him, the officers found a small amount of marijuana. He was charged for that as well. Jerry, meanwhile, was released and allowed to go on his way.

## Confession is Not Good for the Soul

The police had been investigating a series of thefts from a store's stockroom. The manager noticed that some boxes had been opened, merchandise was taken, and then the box was taped back shut. There were several employees who could have taken the items, in addition to the delivery driver who dropped them off. In fact, no one knew when or where the items had been stolen.

The police went to Neal's house and found him outside cutting the grass. They told him that someone said that he was stealing from his job. Neal was starting to panic because he had once taken a box of pens from work. The police told him that they were giving him a chance to come clean and if he did, then they would work things out. Neal, said, "Yes, I have taken things from work." Neal was subsequently arrested and charged with all of the thefts. He tried to say that he only took pens, but who believes a thief?

# BEING SEARCHED

**LEGAL TIP**

**A search is NOT the same as a pat down or frisk. Pat downs don't require consent, but if they ask, you can always refuse.**

# Get a Warrant

The Constitution says that police have to get a warrant to search you or your premises. There are exceptions to the warrant requirement. If they suspect that you have contraband, they can hold you until they get a warrant. There are six exceptions to them having to get a warrant.

a. Incident to arrest: If they arrest you, they can search you and the area.
b. Plain view: If they are where they permitted and they see something that is clearly illegal, they can seize it. If they look into your window and see contraband, then they can seize It and you.
c. Frisk/pat down: If they are patting you down for their safety and they feel something that is illegal, they can seize it. This happens all the time.
d. Consent: If you allow them to search, then no warrant is needed.
e. Automobiles: Unlike most homes, cars are mobile. Thus, the laws are slightly different. If police have probable cause to believe there is contraband in your vehicle, they can search only those places that might contain what

they are looking for. If they are looking for a body, there is no need to search the glove compartment.

f. Hot pursuit: If they are chasing you and you run into a house, they can search you and the area.

# Don't agree to be searched

You can't fight them off if they go ahead and do it, but NEVER consent to being searched. Tell them that you do not agree to being searched and are not consenting, but you are not going to physically resist. I think this can be called the "no rule." The answer is "NO."

18

# Use your words

Silence has been found to be acquiescence, so speak up and say "No." If they say, "Can I search you?" and you are silent, it will be viewed as a form of consent. Quote Nancy Reagan, and just say "no." If they start walking into your house, say "no." Use your words to express your dissent or rather use your one word: NO.

# You can always revoke your consent

Perhaps you gave consent, but now regret it. Well, you can take it back UNLESS they have found something, then it is too late. You can always say, "I changed my mind and I want you to stop." If for some reason you have lost your natural mind and have actually consented to a search, quickly regain your composure and revoke that consent. You don't have to give a reason. If you feel compelled to, just say, "I just remembered the Constitution allows me to refuse." That is the beauty of America. We can say "no" to the government.

20

# You can limit your consent

You can say, "You can search my trunk, but not my car." Or say, "You can search my bag but not anything else." Of course, if they find something, well, all bets are off. If, for some reason, you have decided to give consent, and I cannot possibly understand why, then make it limited.

21

# If they ask and you say "yes," they are going to do it

Maybe you think if you say "yes" to being searched, then they won't search you. Maybe they will think you are a good person and let you go. WRONG! The reverse psychology that you are trying to use will not work. They will search.

# 22

# If you refuse, they might get suspicious

Maybe you think they will get suspicious if you say "no." Newsflash! They are already suspicious. That's why they are asking to search you. Do not be intimidated into giving up your rights. You can always refuse.

# 23

# If you refuse, they may get mad

Maybe you think that they will get mad if you refuse to be searched and they find something anyway. Well, so what? If they did not have the right to search you, you can have the evidence suppressed. Who cares if they are mad? Unless they have a legal reason to search, they can't do it. Boohoo for them. Don't waive your rights.

# Here are some clever ways that they use to trick you:

i. They might ask, "Do you mind if I pat you down for my safety?" You say, "I don't want to be frisked." If they do it anyway, so be it.
ii. They say, "I need to pat you down for my safety" or "I am going to pat you down for my safety." You say, "I am not going to physically resist, but I am not agreeing to being patted down." If they do it anyway, don't resist.
iii. If they don't say anything and just start patting you down, clearly say, "I do not agree to being frisked, and I want you to stop. I am not going to physically resist, but I do not consent to this." You don't owe them any explanation.
iv. If they ask, "Do you mind if I come inside?" You say, "Yes, I mind."

v. If they just start walking in and do not have a warrant, you say, "I don't want you coming inside."

25

# Home is off limits

Never let them into your house to talk, to look around, or for anything. Outside is just fine. Of course, you aren't going to talk.

Whenever they are in your house, anything they see, they hear, or they smell is evidence. If it is in "plain view" or "plain smell," then they can look at it and investigate it if need be. That means if they see, hear or smell evidence that suggests a crime, they can stay and look or make you sit and wait until they get a search warrant. I know that all of this talk of saying "no" is scary, but what is really scary is going to court, getting convicted, and going to jail. Now let me say that hopefully you are following my first rule and are not committing a crime. Still, the Constitution protects both the guilty and the innocent.

The big take-away points are these:

- Never talk if you are the target of an investigation.
- Never agree to being searched if you are the target of an investigation.
- Never let them into your home if you are the target of an investigation.
- The answer is always "no."

If you are the target, why on earth would you help?

## SPECIAL CASES

### John Sort of Consents

Just like a lot of young men his age, John liked to smoke marijuana. Unfortunately for him, marijuana was illegal in his state. One day, the police stopped John for a minor infraction. Apparently, he was not wearing his seatbelt. The officer told John that he knew that guys in his age group smoked weed. John laughed and said, "Of course we do. It should be legalized."

The officer told John that based on what he had just said, "I have probable cause to search your car, so you don't mind if I search your car do you"? John felt like he had no choice and thought that if he refused, the officer might get suspicious. He agreed to the search. The officer found a small amount of marijuana in the ashtray and arrested John.

John's lawyer filed a motion to suppress the evidence, alleging that the officer did not have probable cause to search the car. The judge concluded that even though there was no probable cause to search, John had consented to being searched, and therefore, the evidence was admissible.

### Richie Waits It Out

Richie was pulled over by the police while driving his brother's car. The reason was that his tag light was out. That was an equipment violation and he was going to get a citation. The officer asked if he could search Richie's car. Richie said, "No." The officer told him that he was going to have someone come with a drug-sniffing dog if he did not let him search the car. Richie said, "I am not consenting and I want to leave." The officer had verified that his license and registration were valid, but he would not let him leave. Eventually, a drug sniffing dog unit arrived and the dog alerted them that there were drugs in the car. Richie explained that it was his brother's car and that he had no idea that there were drugs hidden inside. That did not matter; Richie was arrested for trafficking in cocaine.

In court, his lawyer filed a motion to suppress the cocaine, as it was the product of an illegal search, unlawful detention, and an improperly expanded investigation in violation of his Fourth Amendment rights. The officer's only reason for asking to search was because he had a hunch that Richie was up to no good. He admitted that his investigation of the tag light had ended. He admitted that he kept Richie there because he refused to let him search. The court found that since there was no reason to believe that Richie was doing anything illegal that the officer had improperly expanded the investigation from a tag light to a drug investigation and that hold Richie's license and not giving it back constituted an arrest. The cocaine was suppressed and Richie's case was dismissed.

## Brian was a Passenger

Brian was riding in a car with Joel when Joel was pulled over for driving over 100 miles per hour. Several police cars came to the scene because the guys "looked like they might be involved in something." The police asked everyone for identification. Brian gave his, and the police checked and saw that he was not wanted. Brian then asked to leave. The police said that he could not leave and told him that they were going to pat him down. Brian said that he wanted to leave and told them that he did not agree to being frisked. They did it anyway and found a small amount of marijuana in his pocket. Brian kept his cool even though he was angry that the officer was touching him.

One police car was equipped with a video that captured the entire process. Once the case went to trial, Brian's lawyer moved to suppress the marijuana, and his motion was granted. The police had no reason to frisk him, for he was neither suspected of committing a crime nor was there reason to believe that he was armed. The prosecutor tried to argue that Brian had submitted to the frisk voluntarily, but the video showed that he specifically stated that he did not want to be frisked and that he wanted to leave.

# ARE YOU A LAWYER OR DO YOU NEED ONE?

**PRACTICE TIP**

**In law school, they taught us: "He who has himself for a lawyer, has a fool for a client." Lawyers in trouble get a lawyer. Think about that!**

26

# You don't know the law

If you think that you know the law, you don't. I don't care what website or book you read. More people make the absolutely idiotic mistake of thinking that they can argue the law themselves. NO! Law school lasts three intensive years, and then you have to pass the bar exam before you can practice law. An old lawyer knows more law than a new lawyer, and both know more law than you or some Internet lawyer wannabe.

# Jailhouse lawyers suck

If you are in jail and someone else in jail tells you what you should do, don't forget that they are in jail too. There is nothing funnier, and at the same time tragic, than the guy who has been in jail thinking that his time in the law library has qualified him to discuss the finer points of the law. Here's the thing, if that guy is still in jail, then he clearly has not gotten it all figured out yet. If jailhouse lawyers have not gotten their case reversed, the evidence suppressed, the case dismissed, or won at trial, chances are pretty good that they don't know what they are talking about. Just because they can say "Habeas Corpus" does not mean the know how to do it.

28

# Mommy does not have a law degree

If your friend or relative, who is not a lawyer, tells you what the law says, they are probably wrong. I said "probably" because I don't want to insult your mama. But seriously, your mom who is not a lawyer does not know the law, and neither does your uncle. Everybody in your family is going to try to tell you what the law is and what the rules are, but they are usually just wrong about the law itself, its application or its implications. Hire a real lawyer.

# Get a lawyer

You need to hire the best lawyer that you can afford. If you are the target of an investigation, have been charged, or are wanted, then yes, you need a lawyer. Exception: You don't have the right to a lawyer when being investigated for DUI. Also, the police don't have to wait on your lawyer before they can exercise a search warrant or arrest warrant. You can still get a lawyer on your DUI case. In case you were wondering, no, don't take those sobriety tests. Come on, you should have guessed that by now.

# 30

# What your lawyer says cannot be used against you

Get a lawyer to do your talking. There are some limits to this rule, but a lawyer knows them. As I tell my clients, "What you say can and will be used against you, but what I say is not evidence." Let the lawyer do the talking and maybe you can keep walking on this side of freedom.

21

# A good lawyer is not a magician

No lawyer can change the facts. See rule number one, two and three. Don't do it alone, with someone, or armed. People seem to think that if they pay a lot of money to a lawyer that somehow means that they should win their case. Well, sorry to burst your bubble, but that is not the case. A good lawyer helps, but lawyers don't heal the sick, make the blind to see or turn great prosecution cases into garbage. Be realistic.

# Tell your lawyer the truth

A fool tries to represent himself, but a bigger fool lies to his lawyer. I have had clients to lie to me, and boy, it made a mess of things. Would you lie to your doctor? I mean, who goes to the doctor suffering from intense stomach pains and says, "Everything is fine"? No one does that. If you go to the doctor, you tell the doctor what is wrong so that he or she can help fix the issue. Well, lawyers are like doctors of the courtroom. If you lie to us, we can't fix anything. In fact, we might break something. Don't ever lie to your lawyer. At all. I hope that's clear.

33

# Talk to your lawyer

Asking your lawyer why they did or did not do something is a good idea. You can tell them your concerns, tell them what you want done and tell them what you hope the outcome to be, but if you are trying to tell them the law, you are out of your mind. Remember, just because you want it does not mean that you will get it.

## PERSONAL OBSERVATIONS

I am surprised by how many people hire lawyers and then promptly sabotage their whole case by lying to, arguing with, and second guessing their lawyer. Attorneys are duty-bound to represent the best interest of their clients. No lawyer is going to trash your case intentionally because he or she is disloyal.

Hire the best lawyer that you can afford and follow their advice. If you don't trust them or lose confidence, hire another lawyer to be co-counsel. Don't listen to your non-lawyer friends or family as they tell you that the lawyer is not doing his or her job. They are not lawyers, so they don't know what a lawyer actually has to do.

In the end, get a lawyer. Get a lawyer. Get a lawyer. Seriously, I cannot think of any reason not to do it. The prosecutor is a lawyer. The judge is a lawyer. The arresting officer is trained in law enforcement. Everyone has more knowledge of the law than you.

# TALKING, TEXTING AND WRITING OTHERS

**FRIENDLY TIP**

**Once you send it, say it, save it, write it or give it away, law enforcement can find it, recover it, and use it against you. Of course, you should not be doing anything wrong. Still, emails, text messages, and conversations can seem far worse than actually intended when taken out of context.**

# Third party admissions and confessions

Anything you tell someone else, besides your lawyer, can be used against you. That includes things said to friends and family. If you want to tell people your side of the story or anything about the crime being investigated, then you clearly have not learned how to shut up. Your family and peers can be interviewed or subpoenaed to court and forced to testify. Now, understand that if they heard you wrong, misunderstood, or remembered it wrong, it is still going to be used against you. Ask yourself these questions just before you start telling someone your side of the story: (1) how will this person look in court testifying against me? (2) What possible reason do I have to be telling this person my side of the story?

35

# Computers and phones tell tales

If you text it or email it, then it is there for police to find and use. A search warrant is all it takes. Don't break the law with these devices. No hacking, no harassing, no spamming, no facilitating drug sales, and no illegal pornography.

# No, deleting does not make it go away

I know that for you would-be computer masters, you think that you have it all figured out. You think, "All I have to do is delete it." In a word, no. Those texts and other things are just files on your electronic devices, and they can be retrieved. Here is a good way for you to think about how the computer files work. Take a stack of paper and press down with a pen and write something. Now, take the first page that you wrote on and "delete" it by throwing it away. You can still see the outline of what you wrote on the next pages. Well, computer files are sort of like that. I bet some of you are thinking real hard about what it on your phone or computer now. Good. Don't forget that if you sent it, then it is on the other person's device as well. You have no right of privacy on some else's stuff.

# Nothing is secret in jail

If you are talking on a phone in jail, your words are being recorded. If you are talking to someone in jail, they are looking to help themselves out, even if it means hurting you. Trust nothing and trust no one. Being in jail is just like being under a microscope. They check out your visitors, they monitor your communication, they search your cells, and they try to recruit other inmates to snitch on you. Understand, the inmate snitching on you has absolutely no problem lying on you. They are in jail, after all. If you follow the news, you may have seen several stories about how a "jailhouse snitch" ultimately confessed to lying or being coerced to lie.

38

# Everyone reads your social media

If you post it, like it, or let someone else post it and link it to you, it will be used against you. I can't tell you how many idiots pose with guns and then try to claim they don't have one, or how many people post pictures with other people who they later try to claim they do not know. If you are taking pictures with someone and they are not photo bombing you, then you know that person. If you hang out with gang members and get photographed with them, then you too are a gang member, according to law enforcement. No one cares that you have known G-Dog since you all were in first grade and his real name is Gilbert. If Gilbert has become a gang member, then he is a menace to society and a threat to your freedom. Taking pictures with, hanging out with, going for a ride with or being with G-Dog is just stupid on your part. At best, G-Dog needs to be a "how you doing friend." That means that you say, "Hi, how are you doing? How is your family?" After that, you keep it moving.

# DRINKING AND SMOKING

**LIFE POINTER**

**If you can feel it, then you should not drive. If you are not supposed to smoke it, then you should not drive.**

# Yes, they can tell

Bloodshot eyes and slurred speech mean that probable cause exists that you should not be driving. Red, glassy eyes — pretty much any sign that looks like you are drunk or high — means they can investigate you for being drunk or high. They don't have to be able to say how much you had to drink or when you drank it, they just have to be able to say that based on their training and experience, you should not be driving because you were drinking. As a result, don't do it. If they want to take your blood or have you blow into any machine, I don't suggest doing it.

# Air fresheners do not work

Yes, even with the best air fresheners, a passersby can smell the weed on you or coming from your car, so can the cops. Seriously, if you have been smoking, have had people smoke around you, or you have some on you, then everybody can smell it. Congratulations, you are now getting searched or arrested. Unless you are in a place where you can legally possess it, don't possess it. It stinks. You can't cover up the smell with fancy air fresheners, scented oils, etc. I don't care what the Internet says. The odor can give them probable cause to search.

41

# If someone has to ask, then no

If someone is asking you if you are okay to drive or if you are assuring people that you are okay to drive, then you are NOT. Don't drive. I have NEVER met a drunk driver who admits to knowing that they should not have been driving. The law does not care if you are drunk. It only cares that you are affected by alcohol. If you can feel it, then you are affected by it. This is not a test of your ability to hold your liquor. You can kill someone. Just don't do it.

# 42

# You had way more

People who get stopped for a DUI typically say that they only had two beers. No, they had way more than that. Nevertheless, they were not supposed to say anything about drinking when the police asked them about it. Don't lie; just don't answer that question. If you had two or three drinks and weigh less than 200 pounds, you should NOT be driving. If you are thinking that you only "had a few" or "not too many" or "they were small" or anything like that, then you should not be driving.

# 43

# No one cares how close you are to your destination

It is not a defense to drunk driving that say you "live just around the corner" or are you "almost there." Don't do it. WALK. I have more videos than I can count of folks telling the police, "But I live right there!" Even dumber, "But I am already home, so you can't arrest me." The fact that you made it home is irrelevant. This is not baseball. The crime is driving while under the influence. If you are driving or just finished driving, then you were driving. The only question now is whether you were under the influence.

44

# No one cares that you are sorry

It is not a defense that you don't plan on doing it again if they let you go or that you are sorry. You will still be going to jail, and you will be really sorry. By the way, apologies are admissions that you did something wrong. Don't apologize; just shut up.

# 45

# The windows work both ways

They can see you moving around in your car trying to hide something. Yes, trying to hide something means that they have a reason to look for that thing. You still say, "No, you cannot search," and do not answer the question about hiding something. Say "I am not answering that question," and then shut up.

46

# Yes, they can look

If they see you trying to hide stuff in your car, they will ultimately be able to search your car. They will have to get a warrant and can keep you there while they do it. Thus, you and your car are going to be there for a while. Verbalize your lack of consent and ask to leave. It may help. Remember, the legal question is going to be whether detaining you was "unreasonable." Don't lie and say that you were not doing anything. Again, shut up.

# 47 Your car, your house, and your drugs

The law presumes that the owner of the house/apartment/space or the driver of the car controls the property in it. Put another way, if they find drugs in your car or your house, it's yours. If it is out in the open and you are near, you are going to need a lawyer. If your friends have drugs and put it under your seat when the police stop you, the presumption is that those are your drugs. They might get arrested for joint possession, but you are too.

# 48 Friends don't loan to friends who use drugs

If your friends use drugs, don't let them borrow your car, don't let them borrow your apparel (with pockets or compartments) or have stuff mailed to you. If it's found, it's yours. "These are my friend's drugs" is not going to cut it.

# Cleanliness is next to guiltless

If your friends use drugs and they borrowed your car, coat, bag, clothes, or house, make them clean everything before they give your items back. Then check your stuff again. Drug users are not usually very thorough. They will leave something that is illegal.

# 50 Possession is more than holding it

You don't have to have the drugs in your hand or on your person to be charged. It's called **"constructive possession."** If it is within reach or out in the open, it's going to be yours. Don't forget that if it is in the car that you are driving, it is yours no matter where it is found. In a trunk, it's yours. In a box in the trunk, it's still yours. Hidden inside some part of the car, it's yours. Also, more than one person can possess the same drugs. That is called, **"joint possession."** Pardon the pun, but if you are sharing a joint with friends, then you all are in "joint possession." Drugs in the middle of a room is joint possession. Drugs found in the car that you are driving in with someone else is going to be joint possession.

51

# Joint possession is tricky

Just because you are near drugs does not mean they are yours. Never admit to owning anything. If you are reading this, then I presume that the drugs were not yours. If you failed to follow my advice about not being where the drugs were, the least that you can do is shut up.

# The window is not a portal to freedom

If you throw stuff out of the car, they can stop your car, arrest you, and then go back to pick up the stuff. There is nothing magical about throwing it out of the window. Usually, the folks who toss stuff out of the window are fleeing from the police anyway. Jail is in their future for fleeing the police.

# 53

# Putting it down or dropping it is still possession

Throwing drugs on the ground in front of a cop is stupid. You were in possession of them. This also goes for trying to burn them, flush them down the toilet, and bury them. In order to do any of that, you had to be in possession of them.

# Drugs are natural

Yeah, almost every drug is natural. It can grow on trees, come from a bush, be a potted plant, or fall from heaven. If it is an illegal drug in the eyes of the law, it is a crime to use, sell or possess the drug. Go partake of it where it is legal. Use it there. Leave it there. Maybe you think that this drug will open your consciousness to God, the universe and everything. Well, when you reach that holy space, you will hear three words: "You're under arrest." Drugs are illegal in most states and countries.

## PERSONAL OBSERVATIONS

Your friends who use drugs are not the brightest bulbs in the room. They are irresponsible. I don't care how awesome you think they are. When they are using drugs, they are careless. Don't let them use your stuff. I am telling you that because every so often they will leave weed or drug-related objects in your car or your house, and you will end up trying to explain how it got there. I have handled cases where the defendant claims, "It was the friend's drugs." I have never had someone who did not get arrested for drugs come to court and claim that the drugs found were theirs. The reason is obvious. They don't want to get arrested. Maybe they spoke to a lawyer who told them to "shut up." If they were arrested at the same time, some will admit that it was theirs. This might surprise you, but even if they admit it, the prosecutor might still think that possession was "joint possession" and will not dismiss the charges. If they borrow your stuff or are in your car, you must check it. Actually, don't loan them your stuff.

## SPECIAL CASES

### Meredith Learns a Lesson

Meredith was going on a road trip with some family and friends. They picked her up from work and headed out of town. After a long day at work, Meredith fell asleep in the back seat. They decided to stop at a convenience store in a small town. Unfortunately for all of them, the police had set up a sting at that particular convenience store, as it was a haven for meth drug sales. Even more unfortunate for her, one of her travel mates was also transporting a few pounds of marijuana. The marijuana was inside of a bag in the trunk with all of their clothing, but no one claimed the bag. The police charged everyone. Since the marijuana had a distinctive smell, the police said that everyone was aware that it was present in the car and had the intent to possess it.

Meredith spent about two weeks in jail before she was able to get bonded out. It was determined that one of the friends had packed the drugs, but he would not claim ownership. Everyone was angry with him, but his lawyer told him to shut up. Meredith's lawyer was able to prove that she was asleep after having worked a long day, had no prior arrests for drugs, had no knowledge of how marijuana was supposed to smell, and had a recent negative drug test. Her charges were dismissed. Everyone else went to trial and ended up pointing the finger at each other.

## April Learns to Check

April loaned her coat to her friend Felecia to go to a party on Saturday. April knew that Felecia had a slight drug problem. April's mom told her that there was no such thing as a "slight" drug problem, but April and Felecia had been friends since 2nd grade. April was now a senior in high school and was doing pretty well in her classes.

April wore the coat to school on Monday. While she was talking to a friend, she reached into her pocket looking for a pen. She pulled out what she thought was a magic marker. Instead, it was a small glass pipe that was used to smoke drugs. A teacher saw it, and before you know it, April was sitting in front of the school police. The pipe had some drug residue in it. April was arrested and charged with possession of drug related objects for the pipe, possession of narcotics for the residue, and possession of drugs within 1,000 feet of a school. Because she was 17, she was charged as an adult, and she was looking at several years in prison.

April spent a week in jail because her parents could not afford bond money. She was expelled from school and had to attend an alternative school. She tried to convince the courts that the pipe was her friend's, but no one would listen. Furthermore, the friend was not claiming it. In the end, April's lawyer was able to get her in a pre-trial diversion program. She had to complete an intense drug evaluation and treatment program, perform community service, and was banned from returning to that particular school. Felecia graduated with her class, went to prom, and told April that she felt "real bad" about what had happened.

# KEEP YOUR HANDS TO YOURSELF

**PRACTICE TIP**

**There is no such thing as "a little domestic situation," "my business" or anything like that. Keep your hands to yourself.**

# 55

# Get thicker skin

"They pushed my buttons" is not a defense for hitting someone. "She kept running her mouth" is also not a reason. Say it over and over, "Sticks and stones may break my bones, but words will never hurt me." This was taught in grade school but may need to be reinforced in adulthood. Similarly, claiming that "they disrespected me" is not a reason to resist police.

# Your words can hurt you

Here are examples of things not to say:

a. You can't yell "fire" in a crowded theater and cause a panic.

b. You can't threaten to hurt or kill someone. Seriously, so many people think, "I'll kill you" or "I'll kick your ..." is okay. Well, it's not. It is a terroristic threat. If you say it, then someone may believe it.

c. You can't lie about a crime being committed. It's false reporting of a crime.

d. You can't post threats online to blow up stuff or people. If you don't like your school, that's too bad. You can say it "sucks." You can say it is a "stupid" school. However, the minute you start typing things that sound like you are going to do harm to something or to someone, prepare to be arrested. Don't forget, they are going to search your computer, so hopefully you don't have any other potentially threatening information on there.

e. Don't challenge anyone to a fight. You can't challenge anyone to a fight, but for some reason, some people really seem to think that challenging a cop to a fight or otherwise threatening the officer is a constitutional right. It is NOT. Seriously, don't ever claim anything is a constitutional right if you have not read the Constitution.

57

# Do you do stupid things when you get angry?

Don't get angry. If you do, don't do stupid things, such as destroy property. Otherwise, always have bail money handy. If you know you have a temper, do what it takes to fix it or keep yourself under control. Anger management classes help. You are not two years old anymore. If you can't control yourself, the law will find someone who can. I will name a few: The police. The jailer. The judge. The probation department. Oddly, their job is to control people who do stupid things when they get angry. If that describes you, get some help or get a legal defense fund because you are going to need it.

58

# "I'm just hot-blooded"

If you are always fighting with your lover, get a new lover or have bail money handy. All that screaming, fighting, and breaking stuff will get you arrested. Toxic relationships poison everyone. Your friends, your family, and your kids all have to deal with the poison that you and your lover spew. By the way, all of that aggression is not a sign of love. It is a sign that both of you have a problem.

# "It's my business" is not a defense

So many people act shocked when the police show up during one of their arguments. Newsflash! Other people can call the police on you. You might think that they should mind their business. Well, if you are yelling and screaming or fighting, it is their business. They can hear you. To the personal privacy advocates out there, saying, "This is *our* business," "It's *my* business," or any other statements about "business" is not a defense. You can't abuse people even if you are in a relationship or on your own property. Really, if you think that you can because of this, well, perhaps you belong in jail.

60

# There is no such thing as "a little domestic" situation

If someone is hit, pushed, threatened, or intimidated, it is a crime. I kept this short because there are no exceptions and no room for argument. The only way that you can "keep your girl in check" is if you are playing chess.

## PERSONAL OBSERVATIONS

Domestic violence is a horrible act that ruins families, devastates victims' lives, and negatively impacts the kids who grow up in that environment. There is no excuse. If you are putting hands on, threatening to put hands on, or think you can put hands on your significant other, you are wrong. Just stop.

Seriously, I can say nothing more on this except that if you do are a domestic abuser, you deserve to go to jail. Stop reading my book. If you are involved with an abusive person, end the relationship and do everything in your power to put them in jail. Do not show them any mercy. Do not ask for leniency for them. They are dangerous to you and could actually kill you. Treat them like a rabid dog, dangerous no matter how cute they look or deadly if you get too close.

# WHAT'S THAT IN YOUR POCKET?

**PRACTICE TIP**

**Guns, knives, clubs, and anything that is used as a weapon IS a weapon.**

01

# Know your Second Amendment rights and limitations

Our Constitution permits "the right of the people to keep and bear arms." However, if you don't have a gun permit, you can't have a gun. Buying a gun on the street is seriously stupid. Guns with scratched off serial numbers are illegal to possess. Gun laws differ in each state. You have to follow the law of the state you are in at the time. Nevertheless, always get a license or permit. Only take your registered gun where it is allowed. If you are traveling with a gun, know the laws of each state that you are going through.

62

# Knives and other weapons are NOT guns

The Second Amendment does not allow you to carry a switch blade, other knives, nunchucks, swords, throwing stars, brass knuckles, etc. Most states prohibit possessing everything that I listed. Follow that laws of your state regarding this. Sometimes you have to carry them in a case that makes them visible. Never carry concealed.

# 63

# Hiding guns can be a problem

If you are taking your gun out of your house, you better know if you have to leave it on the seat, in a locked glove box, on a holster or whatever. If it accidentally gets covered up, you are carrying a concealed weapon. If you are hiding a gun outside of your home or business, you had better have a good reason. If you get caught, you can shut up (remain silent) all you want, that's not really going to help you. If you are not supposed to have it at all or it was concealed, there is nothing that you could say or not say at that point that will help you. "I did not know that I had a gun" is a hard story to pull off in court. "I did not know that the gun I had was concealed" is also a hard sell. You can try any different combination of words that you want, but no one is going to believe you.

# Pointing a gun at someone

They had better be reaching for a weapon, have broken in your home, be in the process of attacking someone else, or attacking you when you decide to point a gun at an alleged perpetrator. Once you inject the potential of death into a situation, it had better be a situation where death or serious injury was a real, imminent possibility by the other person. In all my years, I have learned this: If you are mad, have just been in a fight, are jealous, or coming back to the scene of an argument and you have a gun, NOTHING good is going to happen.

65

# Shooting someone or at someone

You had better be sure of the reasons you pointed a gun at someone or the reason you pulled the trigger. If the person is leaving, then it is usually not a shooting situation. If he or she has their hands up, don't shoot. If they are running away, don't shoot. If they are walking away, don't shoot.

# 66

# Self-defense applies to right now

You can't shoot someone now because of what you think he will do in the future. The threat must be immediate (now) and real (actual). If the other person is leaving to go to his car to get a gun, lock your door, get your gun, call the cops, and wait. You cannot shoot them before they leave or because you think they will come back.

# Itchy, trigger fingers

Multiple gunshot wounds usually don't support a claim of self-defense. It can happen, but one head shot and eight body shots don't really look like it. No, you cannot fire warning shots into the air. Where is that bullet going to land?

68

# Were they leaving?

Shooting people in the back looks like they were trying to run away from you. That can be a real problem. In fact, if you shoot someone in the back who is unarmed, you are going to have a lifetime in prison to think about why you did it.

69

# You can't create a situation

You cannot start a fight just so that you can claim self-defense. That is murder or assault, depending on how badly you injure the other person.

## SPECIAL CASES

### But He Could Have Come Back

Darryl and T-Bone had a long-running feud. One day they ran into each other, and things just ignited. T-Bone had heard that Darryl was bad-mouthing him on the street, claiming that T-Bone was "snitch." That could have gotten T-Bone killed, so when he saw Darryl, he immediately attacked him. This was really unfair fight because T-Bone was well over 6 feet tall and weighed nearly 300 pounds while Darryl was barely 5'8" and weighed around 150 pounds. T-Bone beat Darryl horribly, and then said, "Don't ever even speak my name again or I will kill you." T-Bone started walking off after that.

One of Darryl's friends passed him a gun and told him to "take care of T-Bone." Darryl ran up behind T-Bone, and when T-Bone turned around, Darryl shot him dead. Darryl tried to claim self-defense, but he lost and was sentenced to life in prison.

Shooting someone after they beat you up is retaliation, not self-defense. T-Bone's threat was not a threat of immediate violence; it was a conditional threat. Lastly, T-Bone had stopped his attack and was leaving.

### Four Friends Become Cellmates

Rita, Bonita, Lori and Evie were best friends. They always had each other's back. Well, Rita found out that Evie's boyfriend, Stuart, was cheating on her with a girl from the marching band named Michelle. They decided to confront Michelle in the bathroom after school.

All four girls followed Michelle into the bathroom and confronted her. Bonita stood by the door to see if anyone was coming. Lori and Rita were talking to her and calling her names. Then Evie hit her. Michelle was afraid that all of the girls would jump her if she fought back, so she just let Evie hit her. Michelle suffered a black eye and a few small cuts to her lip. When she got home, her mother called the police, and Michelle told them what happened.

Rita, Bonita, Lori, and Evie were all arrested and charged with gang assault, which is a felony. Their parents thought that this was just a little school fight and should be handled like that. Under the law, a group of three or more who commit an assault are considered a gang.

# LIAR, LIAR, PANTS ON FIRE

# 70

# Name, rank, and...

When a cop asks your name, address, or date of birth, and you lie, you are getting charged. Tell the truth or shut up. If you shut up, you may still be breaking the law during an investigation. If you lie, you are definitely breaking the law. Just give your name or proper identification.

71

# Don't lie to the Feds

Lying to a federal official is a federal crime. Seriously, so many people end up convicted because they lied to a federal agent, NOT for the crime that was being investigated. If you remember, this was the case for Martha Stewart and Michael Vick, who were both convicted and served time for lying to the feds. In addition, don't lie for other people. Imagine going to jail for lying for a friend who does not go to jail.

72

# Not telling the Feds of a crime is a crime

As amazing as it seems, if you know about a federal felony being committed and don't tell the Feds, it is a crime. This is called "misprision of a felony." The Feds typically use this conviction to get people close to the actual criminal. Don't hang out with criminals, and you won't have a problem.

73

# Lying to state officials is also a crime

Lying to the police is "obstruction of justice," a fancy term for a foolish crime. Shut up or tell the truth. If your friends ask you to lie to the police for them, they are asking you to go to jail with them. No fake alibis. No fake anything. Remember, you don't know what the police know. Suppose your friend was captured on video and you are telling the police that he or she was at your house? Now, you have problems. This is another reason why I advise not to answer questions.

# 74

# Always honor your oath

When you swear to tell the truth, the courts take that very seriously. If you raise your hands or sign anything that contains a statement swearing that it is true, it had better be true. One of the dumbest ways to commit a crime is to do so in writing. It's kind of hard to say that you did not say it when your signature is right there. If you get caught lying, you can be prosecuted for perjury.

# 75 "I just signed it, but I did not read it" is not a defense

When you fill out applications for loans, licenses, or permits, you are saying that your statements are true. The presumption is that you read it. It is not going to be a valid defense that you did not read it. If you signed in the right spot, you had to read something to know the right spot. Sometimes the form actually requires you to say that you read it. This is absolutely nothing like clicking on the "terms of service" boxes that you probably clicked when you activated your phone or signed up for some social media applications. Here is the rule: if it is a government form, tell the truth. If need be, write in other relevant information if the form is or seems incomplete. What are they going to do if you give them more than they asked you?

76

# Banks get special treatment

Lying to get money from a bank is a federal crime. Lying to the bank is, thus, like lying to the Feds. If it is not true at that moment, then don't state it. Period. Banks issue credit cards, auto loans, student loans and all kind of loans. Carefully read the documents that come with the bank applications. Don't lie about employment, where you live, or anything else.

# 7

# Computer applications count too

In case you think, "I did not sign my name, I just did it online." Well, there is no difference. It is the same thing as signing your name.

# SPECIAL CASES

## Dear John Signs on the Dotted Line

John and Charles were best friends. John had good credit, so his friend Charles asked him to go into business with him. They would use Charles' money and John's good credit to buy houses to flip them. Charles was responsible for finding tenants to stay in the homes until they sold, so that they could start making money on the first day.

When John filled out the loan paperwork, there was a box for him to check to say if he would be living in the house or if it was for investment purposes. Charles and the loan officer told John to check that he would be living there. They told John that the interest rate was lower for owner-occupied homes, and doing it this way would not be illegal, as he could always tell the lender that he changed his mind later and decided not move there. "Everybody does it," they said. Therefore, John agreed to do it. John also did not mention that he was getting the down payment from Charles.

They closed on the house and Charles found tenants for the house, a couple with two kids. The husband was a manager at a store and the wife was a stay-at-home mom. Things were great for the first two months, and then life happened. The husband lost his job. They could not pay John, so he missed the mortgage payments. The bank then started foreclosure. They also sent the case to their own investigators for "fraud review" because the default happened inside of six months. After a short investigation, the bank notified the authorities that the loan was fraudulent.

Charles and the loan officer both denied telling John to lie on the loan application. Charles also said that he did not know that John failed to disclose the down payment loan. The trial was short and easy for the prosecution. They had John's signature on all of the documents, and it was simple to show that he never lived in the home. John was convicted and served time in a federal penitentiary.

## Tory Narrowly Misses Going to Jail

Perhaps you are too young to relate to John. Well then, meet Tory, a young man attending college who was hoping to start his own business. Tory, like a lot of students, was low on money for school and expenses. Jobs were hard to find.

Jake told Tory how they could get these small grants for school. All he had to say was that he did not live at home with his parents, and he would qualify for the hardship grant. The best part of the deal was that the money did not have to be repaid. Tory had to give Jake a cut of the money because Jake told him how to get it.

Although Tory filled out the paperwork with Jake, he decided not to do the loan. Jake was angry, but Tory was just not feeling good about the whole thing and walked away from the deal. Months later, an investigator showed up to talk to Tory. He told him that the loan that he applied for was being investigated for fraud. Tory was about to tell them about the whole deal with Jake, but he decided to shut up. He told the investigator that he would speak to his lawyer about the whole situation first. The investigator angrily told Tory that a lawyer would complicate things and that he needed to speak right then, as he was deciding whether to get a warrant. Tory was terrified, so, despite his misgivings, he thought he should speak to the investigator. He figured that the investigator knew everything. Besides, he knew that he did not submit the loan; he just filled out the application. Tory said that he would call a lawyer and then call the investigator back.

The lawyer told Tory that when he agreed to do the fraudulent grant that he had entered a conspiracy with Jake. Furthermore, the lawyer advised Tory that trying to defraud a federal grant issuer was a federal crime, so he could still be prosecuted for misprision of a crime for failing to report Jake. He told Tory that it was a "good thing" that he did not say anything. The lawyer spoke with the investigator and helped them get proof that Jake had stolen Tory's identity. While Tory had to miss a semester of school because he did not have money to pay his tuition, he also missed getting arrested and going to jail. Jake went to prison. It turned out that Jake had been working with other kids doing this particular scam. The other kids were all arrested as well.

# YOU AND YOUR BUDDIES

# Don't be an accessory

Helping someone to commit a crime, even a little bit, is a crime. You can be charged as if you did it yourself.

a. **If you just went there to watch, you have problems.** It is nearly impossible to differentiate a "watcher" from a participant. Going with someone that you know is going to do something is evidence that you were an accessory to that crime. Jail is in your future.

b. **If you just drove them there so they could do it, you are guilty.** It is the same as if you drove them away from the crime. The one who drives them away is the "get-away car driver." The one who drives them there is the "get there car driver." I made up that last phrase, but it is still true. You are the driver for criminals, you are guilty as an accessory.

c. **If you acted as a lookout, you are guilty.** Standing there and looking around makes you a look out. Basically, if it looks as if you are a lookout, then you are a lookout. Maybe you think that no one knows what was in your heart, or your intentions. Well, it does not matter. The question is what did you do? If witnesses say that you were looking around, then you are the lookout. Off to jail you go.

d. **If you encouraged them, you are guilty.** So many online videos show kids encouraging others to fight. While it makes for interesting videos, it makes for great evidence against you too. Since we don't want people committing crimes, we punish those who encourage them.

e. **You don't have to be the main guy to be guilty of the same crime.** Your buddy shot someone and you helped a little bit. Even if they don't catch your friend, they can charge you with the same crime. Well, now you are charged with murder. This applies to every crime and not just murder. As a prosecutor, I tried the friend who helped a murderer even though we had not tried the murderer. In case you are wondering, the charge was murder. Imagine how stupid he felt.

f. **In for a little, in for the whole thing.** Something as simple as telling someone where to buy drugs, who to buy them from, or leaving a door open for friends to sneak in to commit a robbery makes you guilty. You cannot be the information center for criminal operations. Don't commit the crime and don't tell anyone where they can go to commit it or how to commit it, or anything related to any criminal activity.

# 79

# Don't be a safe house

If your friend is wanted by the police, then he should not be welcome in your house or car. That is called harboring a fugitive or hindering the apprehension of a criminal. You can't drive fugitives anywhere, let them spend the night, or give them some money to help them escape or get a hotel. They are poison. On the other hand, maybe you are such good friends that you can't stand the thought of freedom without them. In that case, go ahead and help them. Maybe you can be cellmates.

# Planning a crime is a crime

It's called conspiracy. It only takes two people to have a conspiracy. If text messages, phone calls, emails, and other things show that you were involved, you are co-defendants, also known as co-conspirators who can testify against you as well. Remember my rules. Don't commit or plan a crime with someone.

81

# Meet your co-defendant

If you are part of a conspiracy, you are liable for the acts of everyone, even the people who you don't know. Think of it this way: You go to the post office to mail a package. The clerk who takes your box does not know the driver who transports the box, and neither of them knows the mail carrier who will deliver your box to its final destination. Still, they were all part of delivering your package. If delivering a package was a conspiracy, then they would all be guilty.

# Are you a hero?

If you planned a crime (committed a conspiracy), the only way out is to become a superhero. You have to quit the conspiracy, tell the others that you quit, and, in some places, take steps to prevent the crime from happening. This is probably not safe, as your co-conspirators may want to "talk" to you.

83

# Friends don’t buy friends booze

If you are 21 and buy alcohol for your underage friends, you are going to have real problems. Better hope they don’t get drunk and kill someone.

# You are not the post office

Never let someone send you drugs or illegal things in the mail. That is a federal crime. Do you realize how dumb it is to have something illegal mailed to your home? If someone is asking that you allow this to happen, it is because he or she wants you to get caught if anything goes wrong.

85

# Don't get caught holding the bag

If someone asks you to deliver a package, receive a package, or mail a package, it is your package. Remember when I discussed possession? This also applies if they mail the package to your house and address it to your friend. I can hear you asking, "How that is possible?" Well, it's pretty simple. A package mailed to your house, addressed to someone who does not live at your house is really addressed to you. If you mail a package, well, you mailed it. That one is pretty simple. Like I told you in the beginning, it is not a defense to say, "I did not know what was in there."

86

# Be nosey

"It's none of my business" is not a defense if you are carrying contraband. Claiming that you did not know, did not pay attention or did not look is not going to help you. Willful blindness does not save you.

# 87

# Is that check good?

Letting someone use your bank account to clear a check is never a good idea, especially if the check is stolen. You are the "straw man" or "patsy," and you will be the one getting arrested. If they have a check, they can cash it themselves. They can go to the bank that the check is drawn on or to the check cashing store, or it really does not matter, it is not your problem. Also, if they say that their "friend" or "boss" or whomever will make the check payable to you, then you are a fool if you agree. This happens to so many young folks that it is sad. In case you were wondering, the charge would be forgery.

88

# Birds of a feather commit crimes together

Being with someone who commits a crime before, during and after the crime says that you were involved in the crime. In case you were thinking that you'd meet up there or leave in separate directions, well the only person that you are fooling is yourself. Witnesses, police, prosecutors, judges, and juries are not dumb. Maybe your mom will believe you. Your defense attorney may try to sell that story unless he or she has proof that it is a lie, but believe me, your attorney won't believe you either.

89

# Don't be a storage shed

Don't hold stolen items or other fruits of a crime for someone. Don't let them to drop the weapon off with you. If it's "hot," then you will get burned. If it was planned to be used in a crime, actually used in a crime or used to cover up a crime, then it is a crime for you to hold it for the criminal. You can't take it and throw it away for that person either. Come on, you should be getting the theme by now. Do not help a criminal in any way unless you want to be on the way to prison.

# Don't ride in a stolen car

Riding in an obviously stolen car with your buddies is a crime. A broken window or using a screwdriver to start it usually screams, "I'm a stolen car." If your buddy is driving a new car and everyone knows that he does not have a car, then you should have known it was stolen. Trust me, the end of this joyride will not be joyful.

91

# "I thought we were cool"

Every co-defendant is a potential witness against you. Yes, your friend, your family, your lover, and the guy "you don't know" will cut a deal and sell you down the river. If you are smart, you are trying to cut a deal too. The first one to make a deal gets the best deal. As I tell my clients, "I will sell your mother down the river to protect you unless you say mom is off limits." Any defense lawyer worth having is going to suggest that you snitch on your co-defendants. The smart defendant will take the deal. The dumb defendants who are concerned about keeping their street cred or being a snitch will be totally shocked when their friend turns on them. I have had brother testify against brother, girlfriends testify against her boyfriend, and best friends testify against best friend.

# Better to be a small fish

They use small fish to catch big fish. If you are the big fish (did the most), then they are coming for you. The co-defendants are going to say you are the worst of them. They will say that it was your idea. They will claim that they were scared of you. You manipulated them because you were the leader. You tricked them. The list goes on. Everyone wants to be the little fish. Be little or be first if you want a deal.

# No honor once you are arrested

There is no honor among thieves. Don't ever trust a criminal. If your friends are committing crimes, don't trust them. So many of you have friends that you have known long before they were criminals. They may have been childhood friends or even family members. Sadly, you are not dealing with that old friend you once knew. You are dealing with the present day criminal. To a criminal, you are a tool. They use you to their advantage and when you no longer serve a purpose, they drop you. Don't lose your freedom because you are a good friend. Your so-called friend will use you, ruin your life and drop you. Guaranteed.

# Don’t buy dangerous stuff for people

If you buy a gun and say it's for you, but really it is for someone else, you are going to be in serious trouble. If someone can't buy a gun on his own, there is a reason. Don't help him; otherwise the Bureau of Alcohol, Tobacco, and Firearms or the FBI is going to pay you a visit.

# Beware the crazy fool

There is always that one guy who is crazy. He is the hot-headed guy who is always starting something or does not know how to walk away. This is the guy you avoid at all costs. He is the one with the gun who shoots first and then asks questions. This guy is the one who is going to do something so stupid that your life will be ruined. Seriously, dump the idiot. I cannot tell you how many people end up facing serious charges because of the wild guy. The wild guy is also going to try to sell you down the river. He will claim to be the small fish. Guaranteed.

## SPECIAL CASES

### Michelle Learns a Lesson

Michelle was dating Rod and was very much in love with him. Rod, who had "some trouble" with the law when he was younger, claimed to own a security company. Michelle and Rod went to a gun show. Rod asked Michelle to buy two guns for him for his security company. The gun seller told Michelle that as long as she wrote a contract with Rod that stated she was selling the guns to him, it was all legitimate. Michelle thought that Rod was a good man and needed some help with his security company. She also trusted the gun dealer. As a result, she did it. She bought the guns, filled out the federal forms, and claimed that the guns were for her use. As advised, she wrote a contract with Rod, selling him the guns.

About one year later, Michelle and Rod had broken up, and she had moved on with her life. Federal agents showed up at her house. She learned that the gun that she bought Rod had been used in a murder in California. It was a gang shooting.

Michelle was confident, so she told them everything. She even gave them copies of the contract for the sale of the guns to Rod. They thanked her and then arrested her.

Because she was really buying the gun for someone else, Michelle was what the law called a "straw purchaser." Luckily, Michelle's lawyer could prove that the gun dealer had tricked her. They did not care that Rod had tricked her because women always break the law for their boyfriends. She got probation. She was fortunate because she met women in lockup who were facing many years of jail time for transporting drugs for their boyfriends.

## Henry Cashes a Check

Henry had a friend named Ralph who told him that his new girlfriend had a job and a paycheck but no bank account. Ralph asked Henry if they could get his girlfriend's check made out to Henry because he could cash the check. They would even pay Henry $50 from the money for his trouble. Henry agreed. After all, this was Ralph's girlfriend.

While Henry was in the bank, he noticed that it was taking a long time to cash the check. Then he noticed that two police officers had entered the bank and were looking at him. The officers ultimately arrested him for forgery because the check was a fake.

Henry tried to tell the police that he was cashing a check for Ralph's girlfriend. The first problem was that the check was made out to Henry. The second problem was that Ralph and his girlfriend had driven off from the bank when they saw the police pull up. When Henry called Ralph's phone, no one answered. It went straight to voicemail.

The police tried to link Henry to 10 other forged checks that had been written on that same fake account number, with the same paper, and by the same printer. In fact, they charged him with all of the fake checks, but he was able to work out a deal for the one check he had. One day, he ran into Ralph on the street, but Ralph jumped into a car and sped away.

## What Tiffany Did for Love

Tiffany loved her boyfriend Paul, who she had been dating for about three months. He used to leave stuff at her house, but he told her not to go through his things. Although Paul did not live with her, she let him have packages delivered to her home. One day, an express mail package arrived at her home addressed to Paul and Tiffany accepted the package. Tiffany did not know that the delivery man was an under-cover cop.

A few minutes after delivery, police banged on her door and said that they had a search warrant. They broke in her door because she was taking too long to open the door. She was handcuffed while they went upstairs and searched the apartment. They found a box in one of her closets containing cocaine. They found another box containing marijuana. They then told Tiffany that the package that she accepted contained more drugs.

Tiffany tried to convince the police that she did not know anything about the drugs in her house or the package and that her boyfriend really did not live with her. Police told her that she had just signed for his package and told the undercover officer that her boyfriend did live there. She tried to explain to them that her boyfriend told her to never to look in his things, therefore so she didn't know that there were drugs in his things. As the officer was placing the handcuffs on her, he told her, "Come on, we are not that stupid."

Tiffany's boyfriend heard about her arrest, and he disappeared. The police were really not looking for him because they could never connect him to the drugs. Tiffany spent several months in jail until she was able to post bond. Afterwards was able to negotiate a deal on State charges and not Federal charges.

# WHERE DID YOU GET THAT?

96

# There are many ways to be a thief

Here are some examples:

a. Taking something that is not yours is theft. Hopefully, you knew this already.

b. If you find it lying around, it belongs to someone. Don't take it. Turn it in.

c. If you have to trick someone to get them to give it to you, it is fraud, a form of theft. You have seen where people falsely claim to have cancer in order to get people to give them donations. Well, it does not have to be that elaborate for it to be theft.

d. Buying property that you "should have known" was stolen is theft. If you get expensive items at a ridiculously cheap price from "a guy," then you should have known that it was stolen. If it has tags on it and they are selling it in the parking lot of the store it came from, they probably just stole it. Congratulations, you have received stolen property. In this day of all of the websites and apps wherein people buy and sell things in private transactions, you had better keep screenshots and emails to prove that you bought your items from someone at a reasonable price or that the seller justified the bargain basement price. I have saved several people from jail by getting this information.

# SEX CRIMES

# No such thing as chemical romance

If you have to give her something to make her relax, make her sleep, or otherwise help you to get a "yes," it is rape. It's not cool, not funny, nor just having a little fun. It is a serious crime.

# No drunken consent

If she's drunk, then she is not consenting. If you are both drunk, she is not consenting. You can be an idiot and go ahead, but not only will you be in jail, but you will also gain a real understanding of how it feels to have someone not take "no" for an answer when the topic is sex with you.

# If she's not awake, it's a "no"

If she is not awake, or asleep, unconscious, incapacitated, checked out, limp, or whatever says she's not fully aware of and agreeing to what is happening, then the answer is "NO." It is NOT maybe. It is NOT, she said "yes" before. It is NOT, she would want it. It is just NO, NO, NO!

100

# If she did not say "yes" or you had to pressure her to give in, it is "no"

This cannot be over emphasized. "I thought she was okay with it," "but she did not say anything" or "I know she wanted it" are all phrases that convicted defendants and current registered sex offenders say. It is rape.

# 101

# Force is not just violence

Do not let the "force" be with you. Your so-called "powers of persuasion" are just force. Force does not mean violence, but it does include violence. She does not have to fight you. She does not have to be injured. You don't have to threaten her. It just has to be without her freely given, un-coerced, unforced, voluntary, self initiated consent. I put several men in prison who did not grasp that concept.

# 102 Ways to go to jail for rape

Pressuring her to say "yes" is force. Threatening or intimidating her to make her say "yes" is force. Doing something to stop her from saying "no" is force. Getting her to just be quiet and anything like that is all force. She just keeps quiet and does not say anything is likely the result of force.

Force is rape. You go to jail. Period. So many guys think that there is some wiggle room here. There is none. If she said "no" at first, call it a night. If she says "no" just when you start, it is over. If she says "no" in the middle, that ends it. Her "no" is not to be messed with or challenged. Go for a run to exert the pent up energy, but do not have sexual contact with her at all. No touching, grabbing or contact of any kind.

103

# "I was just playing" is not a defense

Perhaps you think that what you are doing is a joke. Maybe you want to see how far you can get. Well, you will get on the fast track straight to jail. There is no joke that involves touching someone sexually. It does not matter if others are laughing. Don't do it. Don't touch breasts, buttocks, private parts, inner thighs, or expose yourself to women. Don't pull a woman's clothes down or off to expose her body. If you think that it is funny, go and get some psychological help. Stop reading, and go right now. You have a problem. Seriously, I'm not joking.

104

# Underage people are *absolutely* off limits

This applies even if you two are the same age. The law is unforgiving, as it should be. Likewise, society is unforgiving, as it should be. Under the law, an underage person cannot give consent to sexual activity. It is legally impossible for them to say "yes." If for some reason you are talking with an underage person about having some form of sexual contact, given there is absolutely no good reason to have such a conversation, just remember these points: (1) It is always "NO." (2) It can never be "yes." (3) You can go to jail just for having the conversation. (4) You should go to jail for having that conversation.

105

# Show me the birth certificate

a. **Her lie, your jail sentence.** Just because she says she's old enough doesn't make it true. Seriously, she can lie to you about her age and you still go to jail. These types of crimes are what the law calls "strict liability" offenses. That means the law does not care what you intended. If you did the act, then you are guilty.

b. **Looks are deceiving.** "She looked older" is not a defense. A kid is a kid. Mature looking under-aged people are under-aged. Period. Remember, this is a strict liability crime. The law is strict on these offenses.

c. **Show me your degree**. If she isn't in college with proof, then she is in high school or lower and therefore off limits. Better safe than sorry. Even if she lied and faked the documents, you are under arrest if she's underage.

d. **Delete is your friend.** If she/he texted you sexy photos but the person is underage, congratulations, you now possess child porn. You will go to jail. Delete it. Your reply is, "Don't send that to me." Block them if needed. You can control what happens with your phone, but if someone else gets the minor's phone and sees those inappropriate photos sent to you, then you will be looking into the unforgiving eyes of an angry parent and a sex crimes detective.

e. **Do not share.** If you forward photos of an under-aged person's naked photos, then you have distributed child porn — even if you are the same age. I know you may want to show your friends or post the images online, but rest assured, it will be tracked back to you and then your life is going to change drastically and not in a good way. I am going to now go through the questions forming in your head: "But what if..." or "Suppose..." or "How about..."? I am pretty sure most of your questions begin that way. My singular answer to each of your questions is "no, it does not matter."

f. **Do not return the favor.** If you send sexy pictures of yourself to an under-aged person, imagine how sexy you will look in prison scrubs. You can then share sexy selfies with your cell mate. If you are older and sending a younger person sexy photos, then you belong in jail. I really hope that this is not news to you, and I also hope that you have never done this.

g. **"But I'm a kid, too."** It is not a defense to having child porn that you are also under-aged. It does not even matter that you are the same age. "We are in the same grade" is not going to help you either. You may find that hard to believe and I could provide a lengthy explanation, but in the end, whether you like it or not, don't have nude, semi-nude or any photos depicting a minor in sexually suggestive poses. A 15-year-old with nude photos of another 15-year-old is soon to be a sex offender. Delete, don't share, and tell them to stop sending you pics.

h. **Road trip...not.** Don't take your underage crush across state lines where they are considered "under the legal age" in that state. If they are "legal" in your state but under-aged in the new state, then you could end up in the new state's jail. Of course, you can travel with your boyfriend or girlfriend, but you can't do anything that is illegal in a jurisdiction where your sweetheart is considered underage.

i. **Adult special.** If you are an adult and having any sexual communication with, contact with, or even thoughts about an underage person, get yourself some help immediately. Do not act on these considerations. If you have acted on them, then jail is in your future.

## SPECIAL CASES

### Jim Played Too Much

Jim was always a practical joker. He liked to tease people he knew, as well as strangers. Jim was a junior in high school, and he was teasing the new students. One freshman girl had a noticeably big butt. It was huge. Jim thought that it would be funny to grab her butt in front of everyone. When classes were changing, he ran up behind her and started spanking her buttocks and yelling, "Look at her buffalo butt jiggle." Everyone laughed, even the new girl. The next day, when Jim came to school, he was placed under arrest for sexual battery. Because the girl was under the age of 16, it was a felony. A child molestation charge was also added.

Jim thought it was all fun and games. He kept pointing out that the girl had laughed along with everyone else. As the sex crimes detective pointed out to Jim and his parents, the girl laughed because she was embarrassed. She was underage, so no one should have been touching her like that anyway. As the detective told Jim and his family, "He touched a child's butt on purpose. I am not sure how you think that he doesn't go to jail."

It happened in front of over 50 witnesses, so he had no defense. He tried to argue that it was just a joke. When Jim was sentenced, the judge told him that sex crimes are no joke. He was able to get the molestation charged dismissed, but Jim is now a registered sex offender.

## Marc Sends a Life-Changing Group Text

Jennifer, a 15-year-old girl from a nearby high school sent her 15-year-old boyfriend Marc a selfie. In it, she was topless and in her underwear. Marc wanted to show off to his boys, so he sent them a group text showing off his girlfriend. Eventually, word got back to his girlfriend that her photos were being passed around to other students.

Well, soon enough, the school police found out and confiscated the phones of everyone they could find that had the pictures. Several interviews were done and many kids claimed not to know what was in the message until they received it. Eventually, the police found out that Marc was the one who sent the photo initially. Marc was arrested and prosecuted in juvenile court for "sexual exploitation of a minor." The judge decided to send him to a state juvenile detention facility. That is a fancy way of saying "prison for kids." He will be there until he turns 20.

## James had One Too Many

James went to the best party of the year. Everyone was there and drinking. He hit it off with this one girl, and they had been making out in the corner. She had been drinking too. As they danced and played around, she started taking off some of her clothes and doing what seemed like a suggestive hula dance. Eventually, she and James went outside and climbed inside of someone's car. By this point, the girl was clearly very intoxicated. She was slurring her words and needed help to get into the car. James, thinking about everything that they had been doing inside of the party, started feeling under her clothes.

Eventually, he pulled down his pants and was attempting to have sex with her. Fortunately for her, the owner of the car came up and caught them inside. The police were called and James said, "She never said 'no,' and she was coming on to me, too." He was immediately charged with attempted rape and sexual battery. He is now a registered sex offender and currently looking for a place to live because his parent's home was near a school. In his state, sex offenders could not live near a school.

# STUPID CRIMES YOUNG FOLKS COMMIT

106

# Keep your real identification

Getting a fake identification made is forgery, which is a felony. Using someone else's identification is also a crime. If you are under 21, suck it up. You only have 20 years to be under 21 and a lifetime to be over 21. Don't mess up by being impatient.

# 107 Joyriding can lead to prison

Taking a car just to go joyriding...well, that's actually called being a car thief. Stealing cars is a felony. Maybe while joyriding you try to run from the cops and cause a car wreck. You better hope that no one dies because that is "felony murder," which equals a long prison term. You also better hope no one gets seriously hurt; that is a major felony as well.

108

# Keying a car

Cars are expensive, and damaging them causes expensive repairs. Many states make damage over a certain amount a felony. A small scratch may be a misdemeanor, but major damage is a felony. Stick to giving dirty looks.

109

# It's more than just a fight

A fight in a public place is called a crime. It could be considered affray, disorderly conduct, or disturbing the peace.

10

# Who knew they could not take a punch

If you hit someone and knock them unconscious, they will fall to the ground, as unconscious people tend to do. When they bang their head, you had best hope they (1) live or you are facing murder or manslaughter charges, and (2) don't crack their skull or end up paralyzed, or you are facing aggravated battery or mayhem charges. You have the body of an adult and the strength of one too.

# 111 You don't have to leave the store to be guilty of shoplifting

There is something about stealing clothes that young people just cannot resist. Understand that shoplifting is theft, and if convicted, it can keep you from getting job years later. To be guilty, you don't have to make it out of the store. If you stick things in your pocket, in a bag, under your clothes, or in any way take possession of the property with an intention to steal it, then you can be arrested and convicted. Taking it back out and dropping it does not make you less guilty. That just means that you stole it and then changed your mind. Most people, remarkably, seem to change their minds when they realize that they have been spotted by store security. Jail is still in their immediate future.

112

# Getting consent from an underage classmate

Sorry to inform you, but just because you claim that "she's my girlfriend, and she wanted to have sex," this will not save you from prosecution. Your so-called "girlfriend" who is underage may have even initiated sexual contact, but having sex with her is still a crime. Maybe it will be a misdemeanor, but you will still become a "registered sex offender." No one cares that you go to school together. After facing an angry parent or a hard-nosed prosecutor, your life is going to be hard. Remember, no butt grabbing, breast touching, or private part contact with underage classmates. This may be a joke or game to you, but it is a crime. Don't do it ever.

# Helping someone commit a crime

This happens so much that I have to state it again. There is no fast way to make money that involves helping someone commit a crime. I have seen young folks facing life in prison because they helped someone who was going to break into a house. Sadly, the homeowner was there and ended up dead. Now, everyone is facing felony murder. Something as simple as making a phone call can ruin your life. I've seen people who put two folks in touch with each other, for the sake of buying some marijuana, end up facing murder charges because one of the guys shot the other. It was felony murder. It may not be murder or felony murder in your case, but it is going to be *something*.

114

# The hang out spot is someone else's property

If you are hanging out in an abandoned house or building, it actually belongs to someone legally. You can be charged with burglary for being there. If you are lucky, it will just be trespassing, which is still a crime.

# RANDOM FACTS ABOUT COURT AND CASES

# 15

# There is no such thing as a little probation

A lot of young people feel that they will just take a plea to a case that they think is minor. It still goes on your record, though, and you get probation. Probation means that you were sentenced to jail, but the courts are going to see how you do outside of jail. They can always revoke your probation and put you in jail. To prove your guilt initially, they had to have proof beyond a reasonable doubt. However, in order to revoke your probation and put you in jail, they need a lot less.

116

# Being late to court

This is just asking the judge to put you in jail.

# 117 Missing court

This is like jumping off a bridge. It makes no sense, does not end well, and it is hard to explain.

118

# “We are a couple”

It is not a defense to a crime that you all are married, engaged or dating.

119

# Take time to think

If you have time to plan it, then you have time to calm down. Premeditation can happen in an instant.

120

# "It's mine" or "They owe me"

Taking something of value from someone because they owe you is still theft. Just ask O.J. Simpson. In 2007, he admitted to taking sports memorabilia that he said had been stolen from him. He could have used this book.

121

# "Those kids are mine."

If your kids are in state control, such as foster care or placed with another family member in temporary custody, and you take them, you have committed a crime (kidnapping) and will be going to jail. This will certainly interfere with you getting your kids back.

# PEACEFUL DEMON-STRATIONS

**LEGAL TIP**

**The First Amendment guarantees the freedom of speech and assembly, but that comes with a mandatory respect for other people's rights as well. The police know this, and you should too when it comes to joining or organizing a demonstration of any kind.**

122

# "I can say what I want"

No, you can't. You cannot advocate violence or encourage people to commit crimes. If you get really passionate about what you are there for, great. Dissent is essential for democracy. Powerful protests get results. Harsh words are needed sometimes. Criminality is not.

# 22

# "I can protest as long as I am peaceful"

That is not completely true. If a protest gets really large, for instance, the government can intervene if the protest disrupts main thoroughfares. As such, speech in public places can be subject to certain reasonable limitations. Time, place and manner are the legal issues that regulate how expression may occur.

a. **Time** — The time of your demonstration should be within reasonable hours. For instance, it can't carry on throughout the night because that would likely violate some local noise ordinance. Likewise, carrying on a rally during the working day in front of businesses could prohibit patrons from accessing these business offices, and thus the police may ask you to stop blocking the business entrance, etc. Indeed, you may have to obtain a permit so that they can make certain that they do not have too many groups trying to protest at the same time.

b. **Place** — Typically any public place (park, sidewalk, or street) is available for protests and demonstrations. HOWEVER, if the gathering is large or could endanger the public's safety, the police can intervene and usually will.

c. **Manner** — Again, when your right to free speech impedes on or disrupts someone else's rights, such as being too loud or blocking an entrance, the police can restrict your activities. Of course, one will usually know what ordinances are in effect. If you think that an ordinance violates your First Amendment rights, then you can challenge it.

124

# "I own the property" or "The owner gave me permission"

You can protest all you want on your own property or on someone else's if you were given permission to be there. Of course, basic rules of being in a community still apply. You cannot violate noise ordinances or fire codes in so far as size of the gathering is concerned. You still can't cause alarm or advocate violence.

125

# "I am just handing out my literature"

In order to stay out of trouble, your literature should be free, not being sold or exchanged for an "offering" or "donation." You cannot set up a fixed structure for your material, such as tables or stands. That would require a permit because you would be taking up a set space on public property, and essentially acting as a vendor. These rules do not focus on the content of your speech, but on your conduct.

# 126

# Open to the public

People often feel that because a place is "open to the public" that they have special rights there. That is wrong. Businesses, churches, and other publically accessible establishments are private property. Thus, you have to abide by the owners' rules. You can't just go up to your local shopping mall and start handing out things. They can kick you off the property. This happens all the time at political functions when someone starts yelling at one of the candidates. They swoop in and remove the person. If the individual came back, they could be arrested for trespassing.

# 127

# "You can't take my camera or phone"

You have the right to photograph anything or anyone in plain view while in a public place. HOWEVER, If you're videotaping or photography is interfering with police activity, then the officers can ask you to move. Officers can't take your phone or camera without a warrant or unless they have arrested you. With the ability of cameras to zoom in from afar, it is fairly easy to get a good shot from a non-interfering distance. Some officers don't like it, and they will have to be re-trained on the laws. Now audiotaping can violate some state wiretapping or similar laws. Find out what is legal in your state. It is important to note that audio often disproves what someone is saying in court.

chapter 4

# Getting Arrested

If, for some crazy reason you have been arrested, here are some do's and don'ts as you go through the legal process.

# DO'S

128

# Get a lawyer or legal advice

Pay for it. Free advice on a website is sometimes accurate but incomplete. Free advice is worth what you paid. Furthermore, the law is about process. If you feel that your rights have been violated or you have been arrested "for no reason," then there is a proper legal procedure to follow. Follow it. You can be right about the violation(s), but if you don't follow the rules in how you complain or present your case, you will lose. They will dismiss your claim. They will tell you that they feel bad for you. Still, because of procedural rules, your case has to be dismissed.

129

# Get a court reporter

When you go to court, you want an official record of what happened. Always do this, or make sure they are taping the proceedings and that the recorder is working. Without this, there will be no official record of what you claim was error.

130

# Get witnesses

Collect names, phone numbers, and license plate numbers. Find out what businesses were nearby and formally ask them to preserve security videos. You can afford to pay a lawyer just to write these letters. Most places tape over their video every few days, so hurry.

# DON'TS

131

# You cannot write the judge a letter telling your side or get others to do it

The law forbids "off the record" communication with the judge. Say it in court or file a motion. No emails, texts, notes, letters, or phone calls.

132

# Don't yell accusations in court

If the other side is lying, you can't yell out "liar" in court. That is not how it is done.

133

# Don't intimidate witnesses

You can't "get them" back outside of court for what they did or said in court. That is a crime. Intimidating witnesses and paying witnesses off are illegal. If the judge believes their "lies" and rules against you, file an appeal. Follow the rules.

124

# Don't do it yourself; In the end, hire a lawyer

There are so many rules, laws, procedures, and exceptions to them that you are not going to do a good job trying to learn everything and use them intelligently. The prosecutor is a lawyer, so they will beat you with experience.

135

# Don't file stupid complaints

Maybe you feel that the judge, lawyer, prosecutor, police officer or whomever treated you unfairly. Chances are that you just don't understand the rules, but you get all riled up and start filing complaints in the middle of your case. You *are* going to lose credibility, get frustrated, and ultimately lose your case. If your rights were violated, file whatever complaint that you need to with the proper authorities — usually after the case. Before you do, run it by someone who actually knows the rules. We call that person a lawyer.

# Hopefully, you will find the rules that I outlined to be helpful.

Remember, not every person that claims to be a victim is one. Not everyone that is arrested is guilty. Courts litigate to find out who is a victim and who is guilty. Your job is to be smart and KEEP YOUR A$$ OUT OF JAIL.

# About the Author

Kirby Clements Jr. was born in Atlanta, GA, but he grew up all over the East Coast while his father went to dental school before returning to Atlanta. He is a graduate of Oral Roberts University with a degree in history. He obtained his law degree from Emory University School of Law in 1990, and was admitted to the bar that same year. He is licensed to practice law in Georgia, New York and the District of Columbia. He is the senior partner at the Clements Law Group, LLC.

Kirby began his career as a prosecutor in the City of Atlanta Municipal Court, and then moved on to the Dekalb County Solicitor's Office where he prosecuted misdemeanors. He then went to the Fulton County District Attorney's office in Atlanta, where he handled felony trials and appeals. He then left to the Brooklyn District Attorney's Office, where he was Counsel to the Sex Crimes and Special Victim's unit and the First Deputy Bureau Chief of the School Advocacy Unit, handling school related crimes and juveniles tried as adults.

Kirby has been in private practice since 2002, handling criminal defense and consumer protection law. He fights debt collection lawsuits and sues collection agencies for violating the Federal debt collection law. He has been appearing on television as a legal commentator for nearly 20 years, starting off on Court TV, CNN, HLN, MSNBC, and shows such as "Montel," "Nancy Grace," "Jane Velez Mitchell," and "Fatal Attraction."

Kirby also taught trial techniques. He taught Georgia prosecutors in their DUI and Vehicular Homicide training and the Basic Litigation course. He was part of the invited faculty at the Kessler-Eidson Trial Techniques program at Emory University, and he taught in house at the Kings County District Attorney's office.

CPSIA information can be obtained
at www.ICGtesting.com
Printed in the USA
LVHW081901060121
675399LV00008B/327

9 780990 825746